ALBERTA'S OIL PATCH

The People, Politics & Companies

Timothy le Riche

FOLK
LORE
PUBLISHING

© 2006 by Folklore Publishing
First printed in 2006 10 9 8 7 6 5 4 3 2 1
Printed in Canada

The Publisher: Folklore Publishing
Website: www.folklorepublishing.com

Library and Archives Canada Cataloguing in Publication

Le Riche, Timothy, 1959–
    The Alberta oil patch: the people, politics & companies / Timothy le Riche.

Includes bibliographical references.
ISBN 10: 1-894864-62-X
ISBN 13: 978-1-894864-62-6

    1. Petroleum industry and trade—Alberta—History.
I. Title.

HD9574.C23A54 2006   338.2'7282097123   C2006-906625-6

Project Director: Faye Boer
Project Editor: Nicholle Carrière

We acknowledge the support of the Alberta Foundation for the Arts for our publishing program.

We acknowledge the financial support of the Government of Canada through the Book Publishing Industry Development Program (BPIDP) for our publishing activities.

PC:P5

Canadian   Patrimoine
Heritage   canadien

Contents

Dedication

For loved ones lost: Pop, Robyn, Connie and particularly Bob, who taught me about oil.

Acknowledgements

Thank you Faye for another opportunity, and to Nicholle for editing. But most of all, thank you to Jean, who went through the entire project with me, again.

Introduction

In the summer of 2006, signs of the times were everywhere in Alberta: "Now hiring, full time, part time, all shifts, all positions"; "Class 1 drivers needed. Start now"; "Great starting wages"; "Work 1000 hours, get $1000 bonus." As businesses competed to bring in desperately needed labour, job advertisements were posted on commercial streets across the province or blared over radio and TV. Where were all the workers? For the most part, they were working for big paycheques in the oil patch. Thousands of workers, not just from Alberta, but from across Canada and abroad, flowed into the Athabasca region as oil companies poured billions of dollars into building new or expanded oil sands plants. In Grande Prairie, Woodland Tim-Br Mart general manager Greg Bartolotta came to realize he might as well recruit where the job seekers were, so he put Help Wanted ads in Newfoundland newspapers. "We're just really busy here, and it's tough to compete against the 'patch,'" Bartolotta told the *Edmonton Sun*.

Alberta is blessed with massive hydrocarbon deposits. One of the biggest in the world is the oil sands of Athabasca, Peace River and Cold Lake—a thick, black, gooey mixture of clay, water, sand and bitumen. Proven reserves—the stuff that producers can actually get at—are estimated at 175 billion barrels, but the entire oil sands deposit sweeps over such a vast area that the total amount is estimated at 1.7 trillion barrels, about one-third of all known oil on the planet. The amount of oil in the sands that is accessible through current technology could maintain operations for 400 years, or 40 years, depending on the rate of production, which in turn depends on the voracity of the buyers.

America, the top market for Canadian oil, is insatiable, and the Chinese may turn out to be the same. There are basically two types of oil deposits: conventional, in which you drill a hole and the material oozes out; or heavy oil (oil sands), which require a more difficult extraction process. Most of Canada's conventional oil and gas is tapped from the Western Canadian Sedimentary Basin, a geological formation stretching from the Canadian Shield to the Rockies, covering 1.5 million square kilometres over four western provinces and parts of two territories. At its prime, it was one the largest producers of natural gas and oil in the world. These conventional and heavy oil underground formations were created over millions of years of geological action, capturing a huge energy prize for the industrious oilmen of the 20th and 21st centuries who were willing to take a risk.

So it was in 2006, when the street-side signs told Alberta's story. Oil revenues had enabled Ralph Klein's Tory provincial government to not only clear the province's $23-billion debt but also to amass an $8-billion surplus and dole out $400 as a "prosperity dividend" to every Albertan. Wages and salaries were high and rising. Anyone with investment cash had a chance to get rich. Alberta was the place to be.

Early that summer, Alberta Energy Minister Greg Melchin boasted at a conference of financial planners in downtown Edmonton: "I ask, in the context of the future, why Alberta wouldn't be the largest producer of oil on a daily basis in the world taking us out 30 to 50 years? There is so much opportunity to integrate all of our hydrocarbons and to use that as a platform to also be on the leading edge of renewables. Alberta ought to be a perpetual energy leader in whatever form of energy that is used in the centuries ahead. We are in centuries of opportunity, not decades. I don't visualize this ever being a sunset industry."

Not everyone may have appreciated the boosterism, because that summer, the price of gas in Alberta rose above $1 per litre for the first time. Albertans seethed at paying such high rates for fuel taken from their backyard.

Yet not only do Albertans thrive by the resource under their feet, they also die by it. Just after midnight on May 20, 2005, during a long trip home to Edmonton, a terrible crash involving a bus loaded with Syncrude workers killed four of them at the scene. Two more died later. That isn't the only example. In 1982, two crewmen died in a well blowout at Lodgepole near Drayton Valley. Alberta's energy industry has an ugly litany of worker fatalities.

Such is this history of Alberta oil and gas. It has winners, losers, people who got rich, people who went broke. It involves gentlemen and scoundrels, adventurers, scientists, government squabbles, multinational corporations and small businesses, booms and busts and victims. Here is the story of Fort McMurray, first a frontier hamlet, then a distant town and now a bustling city, always struggling to keep up with the influx of oil investment and labour. And a yarn about Turner Valley, a place that burned its energy riches. Or the tale of Dome, a company that began with a single flamboyant employee and grew into one of Canada's largest oil companies before stinging government and investors in a spectacular collapse.

Meet gentle Karl Clark, who gave his career to separating Athabasca's oil from its sands, and his federal competitor Sidney Ells, whose treks through the Alberta wilderness read like an adventure novel. Learn about Imperial Oil Ltd., Canada's biggest energy company, whose history includes famous U.S. billionaire John D. Rockefeller. Find out about Petro-Canada, created by the federal government, which was sufficient reason for Albertans to loathe it.

Eric Harvie was one of the earliest men to become fabulously rich in the Alberta oil patch, then he spent the money amassing an incredible collection of historical artifacts. But he wasn't the only man to strike it rich. There was "Smiling" Jack Gallagher, who went all over the world working for oil companies but came back to Calgary hoping to open the Arctic to exploration and production. Calgary's football field, McMahon Stadium, is named after successful oilmen. Clay Riddell and Murray Edwards, both Calgary oil investors, are on Canada's list of billionaires.

There can be no study of Alberta's energy industry without considering Leduc No. 1. That 1947 well turned Alberta from a farming province into an industrial and commercial contender.

Yet farmers and other landowners often clash with Alberta's primary industry, and sometimes things get tense. In the 1990s, an ugly dispute arose in the Peace Country between a Christian sect led by Wiebo Ludwig and oil operators in the area. All of a sudden, bombs were going off, shots were being fired and a teenager lost her life. International media began reporting Alberta's struggle with its resource heritage.

The world's Big Oil companies were watching, too, but they had their eyes on the prize in the Athabasca region. America, desperate for a safe, steady supply of politically friendly energy, started to take note of the massive resource just across its northern border. The Chinese came in, too, and so did the French.

Every one of Alberta's political leaders has had to deal with the question of how the province's bounty should best be developed to serve both the needs of business and the people who own the resources. Premier William Aberhart gave the energy industry a meagre start, but his protégé Ernest Manning had a better understanding and set about establishing policy to promote an oil economy, and he became the province's longest-serving premier. Another leader, Peter Lougheed, stared down Ottawa in an energy dispute. And Ralph Klein, well, no one pushes him around.

We study history to interpret where we're at today and to understand where our future may be heading. When famous writer Rudyard Kipling stopped in Medicine Hat on a 1907 tour, he considered the area's natural gas reserves and quipped: "You people in this district seem to have all Hell for a basement."

A hundred years later, Albertans are still venting the fumes.

Bitumania

The end of each chapter will offer "Bitumania," some extra tidbits of information. For example, wildcat drilling was an important part of Alberta's energy history. Wildcatting means that a person or company took a risk to drill in a frontier area where no or little information was available about the subsurface. Maybe there was oil or gas, maybe not. Many wildcats were investment-breaking failures, but a few were spectacular successes.

CHAPTER ONE

Wood Buffalo
Fort McMurray and the Athabasca Oil Sands

AN OLD JOKE SAYS THAT FORT MCMURRAY, ALBERTA, IS THE SECOND largest city in Newfoundland. In Fort Mac, as it's commonly known, most people are from somewhere else. They come for high-paying jobs offered by the exploitation of the Athabasca oil sands, part of a deposit spread over 140,800 square kilometres (an area bigger than Florida) around northeastern Alberta and estimated to contain about 175 billion barrels of recoverable oil under current technology. After the turn of the 21st century, an estimated $81 billion worth of projects were either underway or planned to pry out the resource from the oil sands. Workers from across Canada and overseas flowed into Fort Mac, and the city, not for the first time, strained under the demand for housing, services, roads and facilities. Welcome to boomtown Fort McMurray, bursting at the seams.

In the summer of 2006, someone looking to buy a home in Fort McMurray could find a typical three-bedroom, two-bathroom mobile home listed at $320,000. That's not a house, but a small manufactured, prefabricated unit. A similar mobile home in Edmonton at the same time sold for about $80,000. Homes in Edmonton, the province's government centre and industrial heartland, 437 kilometres south of Fort Mac, cost significantly less than in the northern outpost on the cusp of one of the world's largest oil deposits. Census numbers in 2005 showed that 13 percent of the regional population lived in work camps—that's more than 9500 people. Some workers paid to park campers in hotel parking lots. Others rented whatever desperate accommodation they could find—a garage, a tool shed, anything. Some pitched tents.

The city's Burger King offered jobs at $14 per hour, twice the province's minimum wage, while other retail outlets offered free vacations, free temporary accommodation or bonuses, applying all kinds of strategies to attract workers.

Fort Mac is now part of the Regional Municipality of Wood Buffalo, a huge jurisdiction encompassing 68,454 square kilometres of the northeast corner of Alberta. In addition to covering vast wilderness and oil sands deposits, its communities include Fort Chipewyan, Fort MacKay, Fort Fitzgerald, Anzac, Conklin, Janvier and Mariana Lake. Census figures from 2005 showed a youthful average age of 31 among a total population of 73,176. Of those, some 60,983 lived in Fort Mac itself. Statistics Canada pegged the average age for Alberta overall in the same time period at 35, while for Canada it was 37.6. The federal statisticians said that Wood Buffalo grew 17.8 percent between 1996 and 2001, compared to 10.3 percent for Alberta and four percent for Canada as a whole.

Mayor Melissa Blake said in September 2006 that her community needed $1.9 billion over five years to build up needed infrastructure—water treatment and sewage systems, roads, bridges, landfill, recreation centres—to accommodate the population. Speaking to an Alberta Energy and Utilities Board hearing on a proposed $12.8-billion expansion of Shell Canada's massive Albian Sands plant, Blake sounded the warning bell. "Growth of eight percent is explosive. Wood Buffalo has been at least eight percent now for six years and counting." Some critics dubbed Highway 63, a long stretch of notorious pavement that carries the bulk of traffic between Edmonton and Fort Mac, as "death highway." Highway 63 recorded 22 deaths and 250 injuries between 2000 and 2005.

In a sense, the growth of Fort McMurray and the impact of the oil industry upon it can be used as an allegory for Alberta's history. It grew in fits and bursts. Its growth chart dipped as the price of oil collapsed or projects stalled. But when growth came again, it came big—bigger than the elders and councillors had braced for. Fort McMurray's population doubled between 1964 and 1967, the initial Suncor oil sands plant construction years. It grew another 82 percent from 1975 to 1978, the Syncrude start-up period, a time when people queued at the grocery store for fresh vegetables that arrived only once a week. Then came the biggest blitz yet; it started in the late-1990s and is ongoing.

Fort McMurray started in 1870 as a Hudson's Bay Company (HBC) outpost at the convergence of the Clearwater and Athabasca Rivers, a spot known as the Forks. It first appears in a 1901 census as McMurray, with a headcount of 16. Henry Moberly, who established the post, named it after HBC Chief Factor William McMurray. However, the post didn't make enough money in the fur trade, so it was closed in 1898, continuing only as a transport hub. During the gold rush to the Klondike (1898–1907), many prospectors travelled through McMurray. In 1912, HBC reopened McMurray, and the following year, the North-West Mounted Police set up a detachment with one corporal.

The little wilderness outpost grew on lumber and river transport service, but the oil industry was already casting an eye towards it. Federal researcher Sidney Ells produced a two-volume report on a proposed commercial oil sands plant in 1917, while provincial scientist Karl Clark got the nod in 1920 for extraction experiments. Both were thinking of using the bitumen for road surfacing.

Air service, radio and party telephone came to McMurray in 1924, though dial phone and long distance ability didn't materialize until 1958.

It took until 1948 for McMurray to be incorporated with a village population of 621. The first car arrived in 1957 after an 18-hour drive from Edmonton. (The drive today takes about five hours.) In 1962, McMurray's name was changed to Fort McMurray. Highway 63 blazed through in 1967, and by 1980, Fort Mac was officially a city with a population of about 30,000.

Early oil sands ventures brought men and investment to Fort McMurray, but the plants were small and, in terms of commercial-sized mass production, unsuccessful. That changed in 1960, when Great Canadian Oil Sands (GCOS) prepared to launch its giant project. The size and scope of GCOS was more than the region had ever seen. Supply problems plagued local retailers as the demand for goods increased with the influx of oil sands personnel. There were complaints about high prices compared to Edmonton.

Growth-related issues throughout the northeast led to a pragmatic 1995 reorganization that created the Regional Municipality of Wood Buffalo. Just in time for the late-1990s rush.

In 1996, Premier Ralph Klein's provincial government brought in a standardized oil sands tax regime, and Prime Minister Jean Chrétien brought in new tax incentives, including greater deductions for equipment and supplies on new projects. Couple the tax breaks with rising oil prices and the latest boom was on. By the time Chrétien toured the oil sands in June that year, there was already talk of $25 billion in new investment. Actually, it turned out to be much, much more.

Fort McMurray has become a home away from home for thousands of migrant blue-collar workers who abandoned high unemployment in a bid for a big-wage Alberta oil job. There are so many Newfoundlanders working the oil sands that in 2006, Air Canada launched a weekly flight between Fort McMurray and St. John's, direct to Toronto with the same plane continuing on to Newfoundland. Now, Fort McMurray attracts some of the brightest minds from the oilfields of other nations, such as Venezuela, who take up scientific and executive posts. Training in English is a common pastime. Fort Mac is truly becoming cosmopolitan.

Although there is big money to be made, life in the oil sands can be tough. Workers put in long hours and rack up overtime. Many take the bus from Edmonton. Buses are cramped and uncomfortable, and camps offer "zero privacy," as one worker complained in a media report.

"You can hear your neighbour breathing next door, that's how thin the walls are," unionized electrician Kevin Hukeroth told the *Edmonton Sun*. "Five shower stalls for 45 guys, and seven toilets." Camp meals are bland and boring, he said. "I give up my privacy, my wife, my kids, my grandkids. Our divorce rate up here is huge. Lots of guys are on second or third marriages because wives can't handle it."

Police are hard pressed as well. The RCMP reported a 22.6 percent increase in "personal" crimes (assault, sexual assault) from 2004 to 2005. And the Mounties doubled their drug unit from three officers to six.

Early in the 21st century, Fort McMurray became the fastest-growing community in Canada. In March 2006, a hard-pressed Wood Buffalo council grudgingly gave the go-ahead to a temporary trailer camp within Fort McMurray for 300 workers assigned to a recreational complex project. Without the temporary accommodations, no builder could guarantee attracting the required staff to complete the much-needed project, said Mayor Blake. The vacancy rate, in a place where rent for a two-bedroom apartment was $1200 per month (compared to about $700 in Edmonton), was zero. Estimates indicated as many as 6000 new housing units were needed.

Seventeen-year realtor Lance Bussieres, 43, grew up in Fort McMurray and saw it change from a small town with gravel roads and no street lights to a thriving city struggling to meet the needs of its oil-fuelled population.

"We've come a long way," said Bussieres. "In the '60s, it was GCOS, which is now Suncor. Then in the '70s, you had Syncrude roll into town and then Shell or Albian in the mid-'90s. Now there other plants are coming on.

"Certainly, there have been some changes, and they're not all positive."

Bussieres did a stint in the Syncrude mine and then in information-technical services at Suncor before he went into real estate.

"I've seen the average house go from around $90,000 in 1991 up to $440,000," said Bussieres, who worked 10-hour days seven days a week in 2006. (The average house price in Edmonton at this time was $267,000.) "It just comes down to the pressures put on housing in terms of supply and demand. We just weren't able to keep pace. The demand has outpaced supply. Labour and land costs are higher."

There is initial sticker shock.

"Some people don't come because of the prices," said Bussieres.

"The worst thing would be the traffic and the infrastructure. Nobody saw it coming. We're more transient than I'd like to see. There isn't the pride of ownership. There's people here just for a short time. On the positive side, we're seeing now some new facilities. A recreation centre."

Such growth woes are familiar to other Alberta communities, because Fort McMurray wasn't the province's only oil boomtown. One of the earliest was Turner Valley, going back almost a century, but in fact, the history of Alberta oil begins even farther back than that.

Bitumania

Thousands of archaeological sites have been found throughout the oil sands region. In 1976, Suncor workers uncovered bones from a woolly mammoth, which were donated to the provincial museum in Edmonton. Researchers have found evidence of active human societies from as long ago as 10,000 years, including a campsite where hunting and carving tools were made. Blood on the tools indicates these hunter-gatherer groups fed on bison, caribou, fish, moose, beaver, bear, deer and elk. Native ancestors include the Clovis, Oxbow, Avonlea, Dene, Chipewyan, Beaver and the Woodland Cree. Archaeologists found a 500-year-old Cree pottery shard near Fort McMurray. These findings indicate the region was a hub of ancient human activity. About 1000 years ago, the Cree developed string nets for use under the ice on frozen rivers. They became the dominant group in the region. By the 1700s, the Cree were trading with Europeans in Athabasca.

CHAPTER TWO

Bituminous Fountains
Wa Pa Su Provides the Earliest Recorded Hint of the Oil Sands

THE HISTORY OF OIL IN THE NEW WORLD REACHES BACK TO THE aboriginal peoples, who mixed the sticky material with spruce gum to waterproof garments and canoes and found other uses for it, such as dressing wounds.

Pioneers recorded hints of a great resource in the western hinterland of the northern continent. In 1719, three Cree trappers—including a man whose name was taken down as Wa Pa Su—appeared at York Factory on Hudson's Bay. Wa Pa Su presented a small, blackened lump of sticky bitumen. Explorer Henry Kelsey, the post manager at the time, noted in his journal what the aboriginals had told him: "There is a certain gum or pitch that runs down the banks of a river in such abundance that they cannot land but at certain places." The first European to see and confirm this seepage—in what is now Alberta—was Peter Pond.

The son of a Connecticut shoemaker, Pond did a short stint with the British Army, fighting against the French and their Native allies at Ticonderoga, Fort Niagara and Montréal. He was born to be on the move. "I found tarrying at home was too inactive a life for me," Pond wrote in his journal. He was also known for his rage. Explorer David Thompson described him as "a person of industrious habits, a good common education, but of violent temper and unprincipled character."

Later, Pond joined his father at Detroit to work the fur trade. But he shot a man in a duel and was forced to leave the area for a time.

He ventured into the Northwest between 1775 and 1777, accompanied by some fur-trading partners. During that excursion, he was invited to lead a further expedition, this time deep into the region then known as Rupert's Land, where good hunting and trapping was expected. A group of independent traders formed a "joint stock venture" to fund the expedition and share in its profits.

Pond began his 1778 journey by following the rivers and lakes along the Hudson Bay system until he was forced to rely on the Native peoples to show him a portage into a river basin now known as the Athabasca. Sixteen men in four canoes spent a week traversing the steep Methy portage on the Clearwater River near today's Alberta-Saskatchewan border. The portage includes a backbreaking 200-metre drop. Then the group followed the Clearwater until it met the Athabasca, where Fort McMurray is today. In doing so, Pond became the first white man to see the Athabasca River, where he indeed recorded oil seepage on the shoreline. Thus, he also became the first white man to discover oil in Alberta. However, Pond's mission was fur trade, not oil exploration, so the find was recorded but not pursued.

Exploring the Athabasca waterways, Pond set about mapping and drawing as far as what would later become the Peace and Mackenzie Rivers. He established a trading house on the Elk River and picked up good trade volume from Natives who weren't keen to travel the distance to the posts on Hudson Bay.

Pond completed a couple of journeys to Montréal but returned to Athabasca to continue his profitable trading. In 1784, he became partner and shareholder in the new North West Company, the business venture that would challenge Hudson's Bay Company supremacy in the Canadian wilderness. On a return journey from Montréal, Pond was involved in another shooting. Jean-Étienne Waddens, one of the original investors in the North West Company, was shot in the leg at Lac La Ronge as the travelling group weathered an early winter. Waddens bled to death from his injury. For a second time, Pond managed to avoid prosecution, but not suspicion.

Later, at Peace River, Pond was involved in a brawl in which another man was shot and killed. Once again, Pond was implicated. He claimed innocence in both deaths, but the threat of prosecution forced him to abandon the Northwest. He sold his shares in the North West Company, and in 1788, Pond returned to his home in Milford, Connecticut, to work sometimes in government service, but mostly as a cobbler. He died a poor man in 1807.

While Pond's legacy is infamy, his successor went on to fame.

The North West Company dispatched Scotsman Alexander Mackenzie in 1785 to join Peter Pond. Mackenzie's first impression of frontier life was less than inspirational, and he complained that he had been "deprived of every comfort that can render life agreeable." Records hint that Pond and Mackenzie didn't get along—but the former did give the young newcomer insights about the region, particularly its river structure.

Mackenzie was at the Athabasca River when he made a famous 1789 entry in his journal: "At about 24 miles from the fork are some bituminous fountains into which a pole of 20 feet long may be inserted without the least resistance. The bitumen is in a fluid state, and when mixed with gum or the resinous substance collected from the spruce fir, serves to gum the canoes. In its heated state, it emits a smell like that of sea coal. The banks of the river which are there very elevated discover veins of the same bituminous quality."

The North West Company was pushing to discover a viable route to the Pacific. Acting on a Pond theory, by 1789, Mackenzie had followed the Slave River out of Athabasca to Great Slave Lake and then followed a broad and ample river, hoping he'd found the Northwest Passage to the Pacific. Instead, it took him all the way to the northern Beaufort Sea. Frustrated, he named the waterway "Disappointment River." But it was later given his name, and the Mackenzie River is among the world's longest and mightiest. Later, Mackenzie returned to Athabasca to follow another Pond suggestion, this time along the Peace River, eventually finding his way into what would be later named the Fraser system. That, in turn, led him to the Pacific on July 22, 1793, at the mouth of the Bella Coola River.

Mackenzie, the first non-Native to reach both the Arctic and Pacific Oceans over land, was knighted by George III in 1802.

Other explorers were starting to filter into Athabasca. Hudson's Bay Company surveyor Peter Fidler also recorded bitumen flowing from the riverbanks and noted it "has a very sulphurous smell" and was "quite black like real tar, and in my opinion would be a good substitute for that useful mineral."

John Richardson, a member of the John Franklin expedition to find the Northwest Passage to the Pacific, provided the earliest geological examination of the oil sands in 1820. Richardson, with training in geology, biology, botany and zoology, wrote that the "country is so full of bitumen that it flows readily into a pit dug a few feet below the surface." He was the first investigator to realize that the sandy bitumen came from a large, continuous deposit over a huge region. Richardson described a peaty bog filled with petroleum. "This mineral exists in great abundance in this district," he wrote and noted that the material stuck together as a kind of pitchy sandstone. In some cases, fragments held enough petroleum to float down the stream.

Franklin's third expedition was a disaster—the entire group disappeared in Canada's frozen North. As part of the search mission, Richardson returned to Athabasca in 1848 and stopped once again to ponder the strange bitumen flowing from the earth. His observations this time are considered to be the first accurate assessment of oil sands composition, noting that the oil and sand were not chemically combined.

"When examined under a microscope, it seems to be chiefly composed of minute fragments of translucent quartz with a greyish basis in form of an impalpable powder," Richardson stated.

But, like the observers before him, Richardson failed to promote any significant use for the resource. The potential commercial value of the oil sands was disregarded until the federal government sent out scientists in the late 1800s as part of a national inventory of resources. One of the earliest hints of the commercial viability of oil sands development came from John Macoun, a botanist with the Geological Survey of Canada (GSC).

The federal government purchased Rupert's Land from the Hudson's Bay Company in 1869 and then ordered the GSC to get at it—collect samples, map new territory and assess mineral potential. Macoun was searching for potential rail routes through the Rocky Mountains in the early to mid-1870s and then made his way down the Peace and Athabasca Rivers.

His observations of the oil sands foresaw a day "when man would be busy, with his ready instrument, steam, raising the untold wealth which lies buried beneath the surface and converting the present desolation into a bustling mart of trade." Today's multibillion-dollar exploitation of the oil sands, with its thousands of workers, confirms Macoun's intuition from more than 100 years earlier.

"I found a light grey sandstone, partly saturated with the tar, and overlaying this there was at least 15 feet of it completely saturated, and over this again, shale largely charged with alkaline matter. When we landed, the ooze from the bank had flowed down the slope into the water and formed a tarred surface extending along the beach over 100 yards and as hard as iron; but in bright sunshine the surface is quite soft, and the men tracking along shore often sink into it up to their ankles," Macoun wrote.

And Macoun wasn't finished yet. Surveying along the Athabasca River, he found a small tributary stream where "pure tar" was resting under the surface, and his party was able to take samples. This natural process of washing the sand foretold today's highly technical, hot-washing processes pioneered by the likes of Karl Clark and Sidney Ells. Macoun returned east in 1875 carrying samples of wheat, barley, fossils and bottles of Athabasca bitumen.

With information now starting to come in, GSC director F.M. Dawson noted the oil sands in his 1878 annual report.

The GSC sent Robert Bell, one of its top people (he later served five years as acting director), into the Athabasca basin in 1882 to make a geological study and mineral assessment. His report provided ideas on how the oil sands might be used. Bell reported that the Hudson's Bay Company men collected the pitch in barrels and used it for lining boats and repairing roofs. He also proposed that bitumen be carried by boat to a connecting point with the Canadian Pacific Railway, which was planned farther south.

Bell rightly surmised that the oil was seeping from the deep Devonian geological structures into the sandstone layers just beneath the surface.

Then he suggested: "The enormous quantity of asphalt, or thickened petroleum, in such a depth and extent of sand, indicates an abundant origin. It is hardly likely that the source from whence it came is exhausted. The whole of the liquid petroleum may have escaped in some part of the area below the sandstone, while in others it is probably still imprisoned in great quantities and may be found by boring." Bell turned out to be wrong in thinking there were huge "pools" of oil somewhere underground, but his study was the first real indication that the oil sands were a potentially valuable resource.

Back in Ottawa in the late 1880s and 1890s, Christian Hoffman at the GSC, using samples from Bell, was able to separate bitumen from sand using a laboratory hot-water treatment, but experimentation was not taken further after it was concluded that separation was demanding and expensive. Nevertheless, as a result of Bell's findings, speculators, entrepreneurs and scientists flowed into Athabasca for years afterwards seeking the elusive jackpot.

Next up was Robert McConnell of the GSC, sent in 1893 to estimate the extent and value of the tar sands. McConnell calculated 2590 square kilometres with a thickness of 46 to 68 metres.

The Dominion government in 1894 approved $7000 for experimental drilling, and a rig was set up at Athabasca Landing (today the town of Athabasca, 150 kilometres north of Edmonton), reaching a depth of 335 metres by October and hitting two pockets of natural gas but no oil.

Alfred Selwyn, a GSC director, expressed optimism surrounding the oil sands venture: "If oil is found in large quantities, as there is every reason to expect, Canada will own the largest oil fields in the world, and we will be able to supply oil from Athabasca to Manitoba, British Columbia and all the Pacific states of the Union and to the islands of the Pacific. The greatest market for oil not yet exploited is Asia, and if we have the oil in Athabasca it can be exported from there to the millions of Asia cheaper than from any other oilfield."

Drilling continued for the following two summers, but was abandoned after reaching a depth of about 457 metres. In 1896, a second well spudded in (began drilling) at Pelican Rapids, where at 228 metres, the crew hit a tar sand layer but then struck a large gas reservoir at 249 metres. The well was left to spew for more than 20 years, until it was finally capped in 1918. After three wells failed to find a big strike, the Dominion cancelled the program, and oil sands investigation slowed for about a decade.

The lack of success also led the government to change its policy. At the time, the federal government held complete control of natural resources in the West. Now, the Dominion opened the region to private leasing. Among those to take advantage was the colourful Count Alfred von Hammerstein.

The German emigrant was headed to the Yukon Gold Rush, but decided to stay when he reached the Athabasca area and heard about its hidden oilfield. He brought in a drilling rig in 1906 and got to work around Bitumount, about 89 kilometres north of McMurray. Then von Hammerstein went on a promotional campaign, earning an invitation to speak to a 1907 Senate investigating committee in Ottawa. He also toured Montréal, drumming up both Canadian and American investors. The Athabasca Oil and Asphalt Company was founded in Montréal in 1910, the same year that von Hammerstein reported to federal officials that he had struck oil. The entrepreneur then sold more than $21,000 worth of land to investors. Rumours began floating around McMurray that von Hammerstein had "poured a barrel of oil down a hole, drilled for oil and found it." This alleged charade was pulled off just before an investor arrived to have a look.

Another von Hammerstein company, Northern Alberta Exploration, drilled at the mouth of the Horse River and found a huge salt deposit. The company dissolved in 1912, though von Hammerstein was back in the 1920s in an attempt to launch a commercial salt operation. But von Hammerstein never made the huge oil strike he was looking for, nor did he become wealthy. He died in St. Albert in 1941 at age 74.

The University of Alberta, founded in 1907, has always been a major player in the development of Alberta's oil patch and the oil sands in particular. Its first president, Henry Marshall Tory, believed that the university had an important role to play in development of the provincial economy. A group of similar-minded politicians and businessmen decided that more information was needed about the hidden resource in the province's northeast corner. In a letter written by J.L. Cote in 1913, the group asked for data. That letter opened the next phase of oil sands development—the detailed quest for an effective separation method that would enable commercial-scale operations. That is the story of Sidney Ells and Karl Clark.

Bitumania

The Hudson's Bay Company established Athabasca Landing in 1877, about 146 kilometres north of Edmonton, where the Athabasca River loops northeast, and the village became known as the "Gateway to the North." In 1912, it took a day to reach Athabasca Landing by rail from Edmonton, then a three- to nine-day downstream river trip to McMurray, depending on conditions.

From Cree, Athabasca can translate to "grass here and there" or "where reeds grow." The river, which carries the name of the largest oil sands region, originates at the Athabasca glacier in the Canadian Rockies and travels a distance of 1500 kilometres across northern Alberta to drain into Lake Athabasca.

CHAPTER THREE

Oil City
Kootenai Brown Points the Way
to Oil Discovery No.1

ALBERTA WOULD HAVE TO WAIT FOR OIL SANDS DEVELOPMENT, WHICH was proving to be a slow, painstaking process. But elsewhere, particularly in the south, gas seemed to just pop up all over the place, and some spirited entrepreneurs were starting to find and sell oil.

In 1883, a Canadian Pacific Railway (CPR) crew drilling for water about 55 kilometres northwest of Medicine Hat hit natural gas instead. The gas ignited and destroyed the derrick. In the wake of that find, investors in Minnesota and Manitoba formed the Winnipeg and Northwest Petroleum Co., the first oil company active in what was to become Alberta. It folded by 1885, claiming in part that the aboriginals were too hostile.

John George "Kootenai" Brown was one of the earliest pioneers in oil discovery. Curiosity led the western Canadian legend into oil development in the late 1890s. By then, he was already well into his 60s. Brown was born in 1839 in Ireland, studied at Oxford, served in the British military in India, prospected for gold in North America, served as a constable in a gold rush town, was captured by Sitting Bull, was accused and acquitted of murder in Montana and was a pony express rider. Quite a résumé, yet there was more to come. Brown befriended the Kootenay tribe of southeast British Columbia, thereby earning his nickname. He settled and homesteaded in the Cameron Creek and Waterton area of Alberta, but also served with the Rocky Mountain Rangers, who were part of the force that quelled the Louis Riel–led rebellion.

Back on Brown's homestead in 1889, a Native guide led him to a spot where oil was floating on Cameron Creek, which then led him to find it also seeping from the creek bank. Oil seepage was known around the province, and many people somehow lapped it up for use around the farm. Brown soaked up the oil with a gunnysack, squeezed it into containers, boiled it and used the processed material as wagon-wheel lubricant.

Brown's friend William Aldrich filed with the federal government for the first petroleum rights in Alberta and built a cabin at the Cameron Creek location. According to Brown, Aldrich "found that by digging away a few feet of earth in certain places that considerable oil would ooze out of the saturated gravel beds." Aldrich made a wooden pump to draw oil, put it in tin cans and hauled it by horse to sell to farmers at $1 per gallon for lubricating machinery.

Brown's own entrepreneurial spirit led him to follow suit. He hauled oil into Cardston and Fort Macleod for sale. In doing so, he became one of the first people recorded in Alberta history to market oil. His little side business spurred others to set off in search of oil—Alberta's resource machine was firing up.

Imperial Oil Ltd. dispatched an agent to check out the situation, but the big eastern oil company decided it wasn't interested. (Today, Imperial Oil's head office is in Calgary. Obviously, its interest eventually perked up.)

With Brown's advice, locals John Lineham, Allan Patrick and G.K. Leeson formed Calgary-based Rocky Mountain

Development Co. in the late 1890s. They began drilling in 1901 in Cameron Valley, almost in Brown's backyard, striking oil at a depth of about 312 metres in 1902, establishing Alberta's first oil-producing well and one of the few in Canada. Original Discovery No. 1, as it was called, initially flowed at 300 barrels per day, but it had dwindled to nothing by 1904.

Competitor Western Coal and Oil began drilling in the area and spilled what little it found into Cameron Creek. A community called Oil City, a conglomeration of log cabins and tents, sprouted up and then faded. Rocky Mountain's equipment broke apart. Finally, the deposit diminished and no other hits came in. The first rush was over, but it encouraged a wider search directly related to the later strike at Turner Valley. Today, a drilling-rig-shaped cairn marks abandoned Oil City as a national historic site in Waterton National Park.

When Waterton was designated a national park in 1911, 72-year-old Brown was named its first superintendent. He died in 1916, two years after the historic gas find at Turner Valley came in.

Meanwhile, new discoveries were being made in the province's southeast. Gas was so common in the Medicine Hat area that some people drilled their own wells to heat their homes. But the first major gas discovery came in 1909.

Eugene Coste was part of a wealthy family from Marseilles, France, that had immigrated to Canada. Coste was educated as a mining engineer, and with backing from his father, he drilled Ontario's first large natural gas well in 1888. The well in Essex County off the shores of Lake Erie produced 283,167 cubic metres per day. Coste teamed with his brother to wildcat another well, hitting more gas in the Niagara Falls area. The reserves were depleted in about a dozen years, but by then an active exploration and development industry had sprung up. The Costes formed Volcanic Oil and Gas Co. in 1906, but it merged with some competitors in 1911 to become Union Gas Company of Canada Ltd., which became a dominant utility in southwest Ontario.

The CPR struck gas again in 1900 while drilling for coal at Medicine Hat. Civic leaders were on the ball, convincing the CPR to lend them a drilling rig, digging deeper and finding a huge reservoir. They formed a municipally owned utility and provided low-cost heating fuel to citizens in both Medicine Hat and Redcliff. These developments led Rudyard Kipling, who toured the area in 1907, to his "all Hell for a basement" observation.

In 1906, the CPR hired Coste as consulting engineer to guide the search for more gas in Alberta, and he did so at Brooks, Bassano, Dunsmore and, in 1909, at Bow Island. Some sources argue that the Bow Island crew spudded in at the wrong location in 1908. No matter—the well hit gas at 581 metres and produced 127,425 cubic metres per day, taking the title of "Old Glory," the most significant strike to that date.

At the time, the city of Calgary was looking for gas supply. The CPR now had gas, but no market. Eugene Coste saw an opportunity and stepped in. He bought the city's natural gas franchise from Archie Dingman (whose name would go down in history at Turner Valley), then built a 261-kilometre-long pipeline to carry gas to both Lethbridge and Calgary. It was the first pipeline in Alberta. Coste also settled a lease agreement with the CPR for the Bow Island supply and set up Prairie Natural Gas Company. The company's original investors included Clifford

Sifton, a former federal cabinet minister. To fund the pipeline, Coste went to England to pitch to investors but struck out. The English had never seen the prairies and had never heard of natural gas. Back home, Coste changed the company name to Canadian Western Natural Gas, Light, Heat and Power Company and made a second journey to Europe, where he was able to secure funding with understanding made clearer in the new name. Construction of the pipeline began in April 1912 and was completed in 86 days. A second leg reached Lethbridge a few days later. An estimated 12,000 Calgarians gathered at Scotsman's Hill on July 17 to watch Coste's wife light the inaugural flare.

Coste became one of the first people to become wealthy from investment in Alberta's energy.

He went on to develop the Viking gas field, which supplied Edmonton. Coste died in Toronto in 1940. In 1959, an elementary school in southwest Calgary was named after him. Canadian Utilities bought his company in 1972, and ATCO Industries in turn took it over in 1980.

As oil sands, conventional oil and natural gas discoveries became more common, the issue of who owned the resources was also growing in Alberta. It is an issue that is still hotly debated today. After the Canadian takeover of Rupert's Land in 1870, some lands remained under Hudson's Bay Company ownership—three million hectares, or five percent of the former property holdings. In addition, the CPR retained 10 million hectares, a subsidy for building the transcontinental railway. Other railway land grants were offered to other lines to spur rail expansion. Homesteaders were granted title to land and minerals under the surface, but that changed on October 31, 1887, when the government assumed rights to mines and minerals "upon or under" lands. Anyone who had homesteaded prior to that date maintained mineral rights, and these are generally referred to as "freehold properties." Ottawa then went about the business of selling or leasing rights to the minerals, including oil and gas, throughout the western region. Federal hold on Alberta's resource wealth has always dogged oil and gas development.

Bitumania

Natural gas is mostly methane, but also includes ethane, propane, butane and usually smaller amounts of various chemicals such as hydrogen sulphide, carbon dioxide, helium and nitrogen.

A joule (J) is a measurement of small energy amounts, while a gigajoule (GJ) represents one billion of those units. Burning one wooden match completely produces about 1000 J of energy. The typical Alberta home heated by natural gas burns three gigajoules in July, 23 GJ in January and about 135 GJ in a year.

CHAPTER FOUR

Hell's Half Acre
Turner Valley Gas Burns for Decades
Over a Small Patch of Ground

THEY CALL IT HELL'S HALF ACRE FOR A REASON. TURNER VALLEY became Alberta's first significant oil and gas field—a place where excess gas flared over a coulee for 20 years, scorching the earth and lighting the sky.

Writer and historian David Finch proposes that Alberta's energy industry actually began on May 14, 1914, along-side Sheep Creek near Turner Valley when Dingman No. 1 struck gas at 828 metres, causing a gusher of hydrocarbon mixture as high as six metres above the rig floor. There had been previous finds at Turner Valley, but none proved abundant.

Exploitation of the Turner Valley site, about 45 kilometres west of Calgary, began with coal operator William S. Herron of Okotoks, a businessman with a range of interests. Herron's Calgary Petroleum Products (CPP) began drilling on January 13, 1913, with a 25-metre cable-tool rig powered by a coal-fired steam engine. Partner and adversary Archibald Dingman was in charge of drilling and corporate management, so the rig took his name. (A more detailed profile of Herron and Dingman is provided in the next chapter.) The crew hit gas pockets at several depths before the big discovery.

When the head driller drove quickly into Calgary to deliver news of the strike to company headquarters, a board meeting was hastily called. Dingman was ordered to keep it quiet until the extent of the find could be determined. Too late—word was already out.

Dingman was eventually cornered and admitted: "Oil of a very high specific gravity has been struck in the company's No. 1 well, and the quality is equal, if it does not excel, the finest grades found in any territory." In fact, Dingman No. 1 was spewing mostly naphtha, a volatile petroleum derivative used at the time as tractor fuel. Oil didn't start flowing at Turner Valley in significant amounts until 1920.

News of the discovery caused a blitz. As confirmation spread, Calgary's business sector erupted into a frenzy of investment speculation. Hundreds of new oil companies popped up as fraudsters smelled opportunity and sold bogus shares in worthless companies, riding the optimism of the news from Turner Valley. Most of the city's rare motor vehicles were hired or put into service carrying people out to see the well. Riots broke out at the city's Dominion Land Office as speculators raced to file for any available lease rights in the area. Calgary newspapers reported that police had trouble with people crowding First Street as they tried to get into brokerages to buy energy stocks. Buyers lined up three deep at some counters. Estimates suggest that more than 500 companies formed within a few months, with capital pegged at about $400 million, yet only 19 of those started drilling. Several reports indicate some of the gas from the well went straight into the gas tanks of cars. Samples of Turner Valley oil were displayed in stockbrokers' offices to prove the strike was for real.

Taking out mineral leases was relatively inexpensive compared to the potential lucrative returns. A 21-year lease on petroleum and natural gas rights under a quarter section cost a $5 filing fee plus 25 cents per acre per year. Once the rights were in hand, thousands of shares could be sold.

CPP spudded a second well days after Dingman No. 1 struck oil. Only 300 metres away, Dingman No. 2 also hit production in September 1914. The crew was down to 822 metres when there was a hiss followed by a burst of oil about 18 metres into the air. Again, people in Calgary drove out to witness the gusher. Calgary's financial district was madness. Brokers set up where ever they could find available space. Fistfights broke out. The police vowed to crack down on Sunday stock trading, but for the rest of the week, it was round the clock. Up to $500,000 traded hands every day. In three days, CPP stock jumped from $12.50 to $200. It is suggested that more than $1 million was withdrawn from banks and plunked into oil stocks. Some of those stock certificates became wallpaper or fire fodder.

Soon, half a dozen rigs were working around Turner Valley, and more were on the way. Almost overnight, Turner Valley became a bustling gas town, complete with dance halls and at least one bawdy house.

CPP set up a processing plant and spudded Dingman No. 3. But CPP had growing problems, especially the fact that Eugene Coste had a monopoly on natural gas supply to Calgary, tapping the Bow Island gas field. As a result, CPP was forced to flare off gas, lighting up the evening sky and raising the ire of Calgarians who could see it. CPP was criticized for the waste.

Independent companies popped up throughout the region during the rest of the decade and into the 1920s, but they had no way to transport product to larger markets. As a result, they also flared waste gas.

The outbreak of World War I put the brakes on the boom. Dingman, who was president of CPP, and Herron struggled to find the investment needed to develop more of the Turner Valley properties. Then, in 1920, a CPR steam locomotive blew up at the CPP site causing a fire that destroyed the plant.

Imperial Oil, which had an eye on Turner Valley throughout, was ready and bought out CPP to create subsidiary Royalite Oil Company. Historians note that this event offered some foreshadowing of the future development of Canada's oil patch, because it was common for money-strapped Alberta entrepreneurs to look for big companies, often U.S. owned, to help them with financing. Imperial got busy and established a new plant, renegotiated royalty fees with the CPR, built a compressor station and added a pipeline. Calgary finally began burning Turner Valley gas in January 1922. (Coste's Bow Valley monopoly was broken because of depletion at that location.)

The Turner Valley oilfield limped along until a major discovery by Royalite in 1924.

In November 1923, a Royalite crew found gas at a depth of 875 metres, flowing at about 200,000 cubic metres per day. They pressed on, until a superintendent ordered the crew to stop drilling. But he was overruled—the crew was determined to drill through the deep limestone to find out what was there. On October 12, 1924, the tools got stuck— a crisis for drilling teams. If the tools can't be freed, the crew has to abandoned them and start a new well. They began "fishing," which means running hooks or other tools down the hole trying to catch the jam to release it. Suddenly, liquid natural gas rushed out of the well with a jolt that blew loose the jammed tools—only to have them bunch up and trap again higher up, stopping the gas flow. The crew lost two sets of cables but managed to cap the well casing with a large valve. The valve and casing rose under pressure to the top of the rig. Then, deeper in the hole, the casing separated and the valve settled in place, but gas was leaking around the bore. There was a smell like bad eggs, a signal that the gas contained dangerous hydrogen sulphide. (Gas with hydrogen sulphide is known as sour gas. Until this point, all production at Turner Valley had been sweet gas.) After the 1924 discovery, all Turner Valley gas had to be scrubbed to remove the deadly hydrogen sulphide.

On October 19, things got worse. The crew was down at the cookhouse for lunch when the well exploded. Finch reports rig hand Bert Flathers' recollection: "The gas pressure had flown the tools and everything through the top of the derrick. We watched as a big silver cloud of gas moved across the field." The gas spewed along and around some big boilers and ignited. "There was a big flash and No. 4 was on fire."

Royalite No. 4 blew out at 1057 metres. A giant pillar of fire burned for seven weeks and attracted tourists from around the region, lighting up the night sky for hundreds of kilometres. The well produced 566,334 cubic metres per day of dangerous sour gas and was so wild that experts from Oklahoma and Wyoming were brought in to cap it. Waste gas was piped to a coulee, where it burned with a ferocity that shook the ground, seared the land and sparked the name Hell's Half Acre. Over the years, people who came to Turner Valley looking for work often huddled at Hell's Half Acre for warmth.

Despite the blowout crisis, Royalite No. 4 set off the second Turner Valley boom and raised another issue. The Canadian Pacific Railway had been granted land title, including mineral rights, to encourage the construction of rail lines. The CPR began selling homestead land along its routes to create traffic. Those initial sales included mineral rights (at first, natural gas was considered a nuisance— remember the 1883 explosion near Medicine Hat). But when gas and oil were discovered in Texas, Ontario and Alberta, developing a new, potentially lucrative industry, the CPR changed its policy and sold only surface rights to homesteaders. But, a legal dispute arose, and from 1905 to 1912, some 400,000 hectares of Alberta land was considered "split-title," treating petroleum and gas rights separately. Some of that split-title land was in and around Turner Valley.

The deal with CPP to sell to Imperial Oil subsidiary Royalite included leases on split-title lands. Imperial Oil approached the CPR in 1922 asking for an amendment, disputing how much it had to pay and defining what was being produced. The CPR even acknowledged that gasoline might not be a petroleum product. In the end, the CPR got its royalty. The split-title issue flared up again with Imperial Oil's 1947 Leduc discovery, and yet again as late as the 1990s, when a group of Alberta landowners filed lawsuits claiming they had not been fairly paid.

In 1933, Royalite began construction on a high-pressure absorption plant would run for 52 years. All that's left today are remnants of the original 1921 plant.

Flaring into a small coulee known as Hell's Half Acre continued for two decades, until complaints forced the provincial government to bring in regulation in the 1930s.

Turner Valley's third boom came in June 1936 with the discovery of crude oil. It was just in time to support the war effort. In fact, World War II spurred the oilfield's largest expansion. Alberta's oil output had peaked at 10 million barrels per year by 1942, and the majority of that was from Turner Valley.

But by then there were already signs that the field was approaching depletion. Soon, intensive efforts shifted to more productive areas such as Leduc.

The Turner Valley gas plant continued to operate until 1985, when it was closed by its final owner Western Decalta Petroleum Limited. It was designated a provincial historic resource in 1989 and a national historic site in 1995.

Bitumania

The issue of foreign workers in Alberta's oil patch—a particularly sore subject for some unions in the oil patch today—goes all the way back to Turner Valley. The first strike in 1914 made news around the western world, and workers flowed in from the oilfields of Ontario and America. By the 1920s, the number of Americans working at Turner Valley had become a public issue, and the debate continued well into the 1950s. Opponents argued, as they do today, that Albertans owned the resource and that jobs should go to them. Others countered that the Americans were experienced and brought necessary equipment and investment with them. Finally, in July 1938, the provincial government investigated and ruled that some American drillers had received special immigration treatment. Two affected American drilling contractors hired Calgary lawyer Eric Harvie, who later earned a fortune through the Leduc and Redwater oil booms. Although Harvie won for his clients, registration of oil workers began that year.

Today, unions in the oil sands decry the use of Chinese, Venezuelan and other nationals to fill a desperate need for labour.

CHAPTER FIVE

Herron and Dingman
The Battle Over Calgary Petroleum Products

ALBERTA'S OIL PATCH CLAIMS A LOT OF PATERNITY. VARIOUS HISTORIANS have pegged Sidney Ells, Karl Clark, Kootenai Brown or others as the father of Alberta's oil patch. William Stewart Herron Jr. and Archibald Dingman are two more that could lay claim to the title.

Herron, an Ontario native born in 1870, worked the railroads and then went into business for himself in logging, clearing and road building. Short and slight, he applied his high energy to working 16-hour days. In 1905, he moved to Okotoks, about 40 kilometres south of Calgary, and took up ranching—but it wasn't long before he was looking for ways to earn extra income. Under contract, he broke wild range horses, earning one horse for each three he broke. He used the horses to haul coal to an electricity plant in Okotoks. The coal route took him along Sheep Creek. In the spring of 1911, as Herron was waiting for coal to be loaded, he set off to examine gas seepages that were well known around the creek.

His observations led to further investigation using a wooden whiskey barrel, his wife's wash boiler, a pair of vinegar jars, a length of rubber hose, some paraffin wax and a Bunsen burner. He cut one end off the barrel and bored a hole for the hose in the other. At the seepage site, Herron dug a hole, placed the open end of the barrel over the hole, packed loam and clay around it and sealed the hose with the wax. The other end of the hose went into a water-filled vinegar jar. Soon, gas was bubbling up through the water. Next, he connected the hose to the Bunsen burner, and a small blue flame appeared. He filled the two vinegar jugs with samples of the gas and sent them off to the U.S. for testing.

The tests confirmed that the seepage was not swamp gas, but was petroleum based, particularly full of naphtha and propane.

Herron set out to acquire land and mineral rights. That same year, he bought out farmer Michael Stoos for $18,000 and purchased rights in the area from a Calgary real estate firm for $15,000. Stoos had purchased his land from the CPR, but the railway had retained the petroleum rights, so Herron had to apply to both the Dominion government and the railway for lease rights. Those purchases covered a critical area that included the seepages Herron had been studying. Some historians mark Herron's land and mineral rights acquisitions at Sheep Creek as the beginning of Alberta's oil and gas history. (As we have seen, there are a number of events that could be interpreted as the "beginning.")

Then, like every other oil entrepreneur, Herron had to find the money to launch a petroleum exploration company. There is a common adage that says the best way to reach the top is to get in on the ground floor. Unfortunately for Herron, though he was first in, he spent his entire career struggling with money issues, particularly demands for overdue government royalty payments.

A long-standing myth says that Herron once struck a match on a rock to light one of the seepages, then used the fire to cook bacon and eggs for potential investors.

Another version of this story suggests that local cowboys had been doing the same thing for years. Historians discount the anecdotes. (You can imagine the danger of a large explosion. In 1888, cowboy John Ware was riding west of Okotoks when he stopped for a drink at a small pond and noticed a light film on the water emitting a sulphurous odour. When he tossed a match, the pond exploded, sending his frightened horse off into the brush.)

By 1913, Herron had rounded up an investment group that included Archibald Dingman, an oilman with experience in Pennsylvania and Ontario who was then drilling in Alberta. In addition to the oil business, Dingman had also worked making soap and bicycle brakes and operating electric streetlights before moving to Alberta in 1902. While working for Scarborough Electric Railway, Dingman claimed to be the first person to install electric lights in Toronto. As a partner in a company that manufactured Comfort Soap, he continued to make plans for an oil company to operate east of Toronto. But when the Comfort Soap plant was destroyed by fire in 1890, Dingman went west.

The city of Calgary was supplied with gas manufactured from coal, but wanted a cheaper source. Dingman set up the Calgary Natural Gas Company in 1905 and drilled two wells—the first was dry, but the second produced enough gas to supply the city's streetlights and the Calgary Brewing and Malting Company. (It was at this point that Eugene Coste moved to bring Bow Island gas to Calgary.)

In 1912, Herron sold Dingman an option to acquire 55 percent of his Turner Valley leases with commitment to spend $50,000 in development. Dingman exercised the option, funded by a syndicate that included James A. Lougheed, grandfather of future premier Peter Lougheed, and R.B. Bennett, a future prime minister. The new ownership group set up Calgary Petroleum Products (CPP) and staked it with $50,000. Right from the start, Herron and Dingman did not get along. Herron was required to sign over almost half his remaining interest in the company to pay Dingman for services. Dingman tried to push Herron into a minor role, and the latter was even refused a seat on the corporate board. The dispute dragged on throughout the term of the partnership. Dingman later claimed Herron was overpaid for the properties that were transferred in the original agreement. Herron countered that he was underpaid on his 25 percent corporate interest. Dingman responded that Herron had filed lease applications for himself that should have gone to the company. Herron denied any such arrangement had existed. So it went on.

While this power maneuvering was underway, Herron set about extending his land holdings in Turner Valley. Using his proceeds from CPP, he also set up a series of other oil companies.

News spread that there might be an oilfield near Turner Valley, and the first land rush was on. It increased as CPP began drilling in early 1913. When the first strike came in the spring of 1914, it was Dingman's name that entered the history books. The well was called Dingman No. 1, because he was the driller and operations manager. It was also Dingman who got all the publicity—his name was in the papers, not Herron's. But it was Herron's insight and hard work that brought the project in as the largest commercial gas strike in Western Canada.

One of the first blows to CPP's development and Herron's success was the outbreak of World War I, because it dried up sources of investment. To raise operating cash for CPP, Herron, who had become known as "Never Sell Herron," began a process of leveraging rights on properties here and there each time he needed money. Herron claimed he had spent $225,000 on his Turner Valley ventures. By 1915, he was already in royalty arrears to the federal government. This began a long series of requests for more time to pay or for credit against drilling expenses. Herron's difficulties with Ottawa become one of the earliest examples of western resentment. Early federal policy on energy was ill defined and sometimes ad hoc. Political influence from the U.S. and Europe, as well as Eastern Canada, far outstripped anything the western oilmen could muster.

As time went on, Herron continued to bargain with lease rights and even put up his Calgary home to raise cash and keep himself in the game.

Despite his difficulties, Herron hung on. By 1920, CPP had only two naphtha wells and a plant to strip fuel. Production was 40 barrels a day.

"I knew—or at least I thought I knew, which amounts to the same thing—that there was oil in the valley," Herron said.

However, also in 1920, fire destroyed the CPP plant forcing the company's executives to negotiate a takeover by Standard Oil's Canadian subsidiary Imperial Oil. Previously, CPP had fought off an Imperial takeover, but the loss of the uninsured plant forced its hand. Bennett arranged for the transfer of CPP assets to a new company called Royalite Oil Company, incorporated in 1921, with 25 percent owned by CPP shareholders and 75 percent owned by Imperial Oil. The new majority owner pledged $400,000 to rebuild and drill more wells. Royalite struck significant oil in October 1924, and the next Turner Valley boom was on, yet Herron was now mostly in the background of corporate developments.

But he made yet another deal, this time with McLeod Oil Company Ltd., to drill on one of his most promising leases. McLeod No. 1 hit oil in December 1924.

The next blow came in 1925, with a federal decision that commercially producing wells could not claim drilling expenses. Herron desperately needed the credits, and he wrote to Ottawa to complain bitterly about a decision particular to the McLeod well.

"I as the lessee hold a royalty interest, and I have had the small sum of $250 paid to me for my royalty from the production of five months from January 1 to May 31, and this was the first dollar that I have ever obtained from the field in the form of dividends or royalty since I started the field as the pioneer in July 1911, and I put into the field of my own money over $1 million," Herron wrote. "I, as stated, have put a fortune into the field through my faith in it and enterprise, and have given it 15 years of the best of my life to endeavour to prove that it will be a commercial oilfield and worthy of my effort, and why should the government demand that I pay more and more money in rentals until I get some returns from the large sums that I have expended?"

The boom-and-bust cycle continued at Turner Valley, and Herron never seemed to beat it. A mansion he bought in Calgary's Mount Royal district was seized by the city for non-payment of taxes.

When McLeod No. 2 came in on February 1926, Herron's position improved a bit. He was able to form another company, Okalta Oils Ltd., but this time as a majority shareholder. In late 1928, Okalta brought in a major strike.

Almost 20 years of conviction and hard work had finally brought Herron a measure of success. He was even able to pay off his city tax bill to regain the Mount Royal mansion.

In 1930, Alberta took over control of provincial resources, and Herron found himself an advocate for independent producers against major players such as Imperial Oil. In July 1938, debate between the government and various parties including Herron led to the creation of the Conservation Board, the precursor of today's Alberta Energy and Utilities Board.

The 70-year-old Herron was on a Turner Valley derrick floor in 1939, when he collapsed from a stroke and died in a Calgary hospital a few weeks later. After his death, Okalta No. 7 and No. 8 came in. Okalta continued under Herron's son until 1970, when it was reorganized into Oakwood Petroleum Ltd.

Dingman continued working right up until his death at 85, leaving a plan for two decades of further oil exploration. He is remembered for his favourite slogan: "Carry on, we want and need more crude oil."

Bitumania

William Herron's best year was 1928. After a dispute with Archie Dingman and Calgary Petroleum Products, Herron's own firm Okalta Oils hit the front pages in November. Okalta No. 1, drilling on a spot Herron had purchased 16 years earlier, struck a reservoir that proved a flow of 906,735 cubic metres per day, yielding more than 1000 barrels of gasoline per day. The *Calgary Herald* report included a photo of the 61-metre-high Okalta gas flare and derrick. Okalta's preferred shares had been offered on the first of the month with no buyers at $66. After the strike, they were selling for $345 and closed at the end of November at

$367.50 each. With only two months' production at year-end, Okalta had become Turner Valley's largest producer.

CHAPTER SIX

Sidney Ells
A Poet and Sketch Artist Explores the Oil Sands

IN THE SAME YEAR THAT DRILLING BEGAN AT TURNER VALLEY, A YOUNG Ottawa scientist arrived in McMurray to begin a 32-year, career-long study of the Athabasca oil sands. Sidney Ells held degrees in arts and science. He had been a miner in Nova Scotia, a surveyor and a maintenance engineer for the Grand Trunk rail line.

Ells was assistant to the director of the Mines Branch in Ottawa when a letter of inquiry arrived from a group of Albertans. Written by politician Jean Cote, it required more information about the northeast Alberta oil sands. The inquiry was passed to Ells, who did a survey of research only to discover there was very little other than some information from the 1883 Geological Survey of Canada excursion. Ells wrote: "The assumption was made that the sands extended over an area of 1000 square miles, and that the average thickness was 200 feet; as a result, the estimated bitumen content reached astronomical proportions."

Eager to see the oil sands, Ells accordingly requested permission for a field study at Athabasca. "The first step had been taken on a long, long trail, which over many years was to lead to almost every hardship that can be encountered in the North," he recalled later in a 1962 federal information circular. Ells was a skilful sketch artist and amateur poet. His drawings bring to life the difficulty of his journeys into the northern wilderness and the bleak oil sands plant sites that cut into the wilderness. He was also known for keeping excellent records; however, his methodology came into question.

At a time when McMurray was in the middle of nowhere, the only way in was on foot and by river, usually on a scow (a wide, flat-bottomed boat built to carry a large load of supplies). Scows often got stuck or struggled upstream. In such cases, crews known as "trackers" walked the shoreline, using ropes to pull the boats along. It was brutal work. One Ells sketch depicts bulky men straining forward against leather straps as they pull.

"Drifting day and night with a three-mile current and with only a lookout on duty, we reached and portaged past Grand Rapids on the third day and on the ninth day reached McMurray," Ells wrote.

In 1913, Ells first arrived in McMurray, a collection of log cabins with no rail, no road, no telegraph. McMurray received mail four times a year, by river in summer and by dog train in winter. Ells called the one hotel there a "bug-infested hovel" and noted that starving train dogs roamed at will. Perishable goods were precious. Salt, sugar and other staples sold for three pounds for a dollar, so McMurray was known as a "three-for-a-dollar" settlement.

Ells' circular describes reconnaissance over an "aggregate" 298 kilometres. That included an area about 60 kilometres southwest of McMurray where he found a 47-metre bituminous sand exposure plus another section 160 kilometres north of town along the Athabasca River. And he explored eight tributary streams including the Firebag, Clearwater and Christina. Ells counted 247 bituminous outcroppings, of which he photographed and measured 80.

"Augers and extension rods, hand tools and explosives were carried in the canoe, and more than 200 individual samples were secured at depths of from five to 17 feet and packed in friction top tins," Ells reported. "Where conditions indicated that unaltered material might be reached at reasonable depth, a number of the holes were loaded and fired and sacks of representative bulk samples secured." Eventually some 1200 sacks, each capable of holding 45 kilograms, were filled with oil sand, hauled in scows to McMurray, and stored in a roughly constructed log storehouse.

His return trip to Edmonton included 8.2 tonnes of equipment and samples. The crew was mostly aboriginal men who initially declined to help track the scow, until the local RCMP officer took up a line and called to the men in their own language.

Ells claims his 1913 specimens were "the first true samples of oil sands" brought out for testing and examination. It took the large scow and tracking crew 23 days (17 of which were ridden with snow or rain) to reach Athabasca Landing.

"Breakfast was eaten by firelight; we pulled on the line until dark and then, lacking tents, slept under the dripping trees," Ells noted. Three men were downed by hernia, appendicitis or pneumonia and took a place in the makeshift sick bay at the bottom of the scow.

"Thereafter I took a place on the tracking line," said Ells.

Because of government budget constraints, Ells, who earned $1800 a year, was forced to pay part of the trackers' wages from his own pocket. A tracker was paid $45 one way, plus tobacco and moccasins. "It was an immutable custom that they be provided with moccasins and tobacco, and I had therefore laid in a gunnysack full of each at a cost of $38. However, on reaching Ottawa (and having completed a trip that was long discussed around northern campfires) an indulgent and grateful Department of the Government declined to remunerate me for the cost of the moccasins and tobacco," Ells complained in his 1962 information circular. He also stated that between 1913 and 1941, his federal funding did not exceed $140,000.

Despite the daunting insects, the merciless terrain and the lack of funding, Ells was hooked. He returned the next year and hauled over 54 tonnes of samples back to Edmonton. Ells' journeys through the northern Alberta wilderness were filled with hardship and duress, yet his writings make him sound like a man who accepted difficulties with a spirit of pride. In 1914, while canoeing with another man towards La Loche Lake, their canoe was swamped and their food lost. They reached the La Loche trading post a day later, only to discover the summer shipment had not arrived and the trader was living on fish and little else. Thankfully, the rivers were "teeming" with whitefish and trout, a diet that carried them to Big River 10 days later.

Describing a June 1915 journey from McMurray to Athabasca Landing, a distance of some 400 kilometres, and then on to Edmonton, Ells travelled from 3:00 AM to 11:00 PM each day thanks to long summer daylight hours. His notes suggest that his only company was a cocker spaniel, but no name was given for the dog or any explanation for how he got it. He developed blisters on his feet, switched to moccasins, which made the blisters worse, and got soaked on soft, waterlogged ground. Then a cold wind brought in rain. Teeth chattering and feet numb, Ells managed to find a dry spot, shred some birch bark, strike a match and get a small fire going, which he fed with alder that was growing nearby. "It's amazing how wet and green alder will burn." Seven days later at 3:00 AM, suffering bleeding feet and an infection, he knocked on a farm door north of Athabasca and nearly had the door slammed in his face. Ells begged to pay a dollar for a shot of whiskey, which he received. The farmer offered him a ride to Athabasca in the back of a pig truck. "I climbed into the back of the springless farm wagon with porcine companions," Ells wrote.

He had another harrowing adventure in 1923, setting off from Edmonton in January in freezing temperatures and darker days. Ells' journey with the spaniel had apparently convinced him that summer travel was dangerous because of the wet conditions in the bush. This trip was an attempt to find advantage in winter travel. At least 11 men were with him, but when temperatures dropped to −46°C two weeks in, the cook quit. So Ells took over the duty, rising at 5:00 AM each day, building a fire and melting snow to use as water.

In another incident, history writer Darlene Comfort reports that a man found Ells in the wilderness pulling a toboggan. The man asked why the federal man wasn't using dogs. "The government can't afford dogs," Ells replied. Beside a fire later, the man shared what little food he had with Ells, who had nothing but a small amount of rice. "The government can't afford food, either," he explained.

On his return in 1914, Ells needed a large quantity of bitumen, not just for testing but also for demonstration: using the material in pavement in Edmonton. In 1915, a demonstration project laid 60 metres of oil sands–based asphalt along Kinnaird Street. However, Ells hurt his credibility by going ahead with the paving demonstration without heeding instructions from City of Edmonton engineers, straining relations between the Mines Branch and the city. Ells was censured for the mistake.

Paving materials from oil sands product were also used in Ottawa, Jasper, Medicine Hat and Camrose. However, realization was growing that oil sands had greater potential as a fuel source.

Despite the Edmonton incident, Ells, also in 1915, was able to convince his employer to pay for a research stint at the Mellon Institute of Industrial Research in Pittsburgh. There, under guidance from experts in engineering, chemistry and mining, Ells studied his Athabasca samples, experimenting with a variety of temperatures and chemicals while searching for an effective separation process. Indeed, his report referred in "notes" to a hot-water process that resulted in 99.7 percent pure bitumen, but no backup data was given. The Mellon experiments raised Ells' enthusiasm about the potential for success at Athabasca. His study resulted in a lengthy technical document that said much about the writer, revealing enthusiasm and self-confidence. His report also rightly pointed out that the common term "tar sands" applied to the Athabasca resource was wrong, and that something akin to "bituminous sands" was more accurate. He called for detailed exploration using core drilling and reported that, though most outcroppings would be eliminated as potential resources, certain areas could still be open to large-scale development. And he recognized that transportation costs were a vital issue.

Ells noted that bitumen deposits had been used since the 1830s as a source of paving material in Europe and the United States. "By comparison, it was clear that the Alberta deposit is much larger than any other known occurrence of similar material and from present knowledge may possibly represent a larger tonnage than that of all other similar deposits combined," he wrote.

The report to Ottawa outlined Ells' finding that the oil sands could be mined and the product used as a paving material. He pointed to a spot on the Horse River, only a few kilometres from McMurray, as the best location for a federal project. (This can be viewed as one of the precursors to the ongoing battle between the federal and provincial governments over jurisdiction in the oil sands. Ottawa eventually gave up control of resources to the provinces, but held onto four of the best oil sands deposits until 1957. The federal government argued that the material could be used for paving in western national parks.) The federal government's national parks branch established the Horse River Reserve, made up of 232 hectares just south of McMurray, and earmarked it for research. In 1920, Ells took a closer look at the Horse River site. "Field analyses indicated that some five million tons of commercial grade sand were available and that mining would involve the removal of some three million tonnes of overburden. Furthermore, it had become clear that the Horse River Reserve was the only area within reasonable distance of McMurray where bituminous sand could be mined at moderate cost."

Finally, Ells' report also confirmed earlier study by Christian Hoffman and Robert Bell, which found that the oil sands contained a petroleum resource, and he concluded that oil sands separation was key to exploitation.

As shall be seen, Ells' submission to the Mines Branch was scrutinized and criticized by staff scientists Karl Clark and Joseph Keele. They found Ells' document lacking, filled with gaps and in some ways incoherent. Clark and Keele suggested that the report raised good questions but added little to the existing body of data. They recommended a rewrite, using scientific methodology. Ells' boss, Eugene Haanel, who was already angry over the Edmonton paving demonstration, wanted to can him. Ells' poor reputation dogged him throughout his oil sands career, and many other scientists, notably Clark, tended to avoid him. Ells, who had originally cooperated and shared information with the University of Alberta and the province, later played his cards closer to his chest. He remained convinced that competitors were trying to discredit him and his research. He complained that Clark, who was to become Alberta's primary oil sands researcher, was capitalizing on Ells' initial findings.

A more detailed and scientific report submitted by a Mines Branch colleague confirmed that the oil sands held great potential, but that it was to be a tough slog, with expensive and detailed work ahead. Based on that warning from two researchers, the federal government was reluctant to proceed on oil sands development.

During World War I, Ells fought with the 23rd Battery, Royal Canadian Field Artillery, ranked lieutenant. After the war, he returned to the Athabasca area.

The railway reached McMurray in the 1920s, making it easier to move equipment and men in and out. Word was starting to spread about a potential commercial oil play at Athabasca—something big and efficient enough to be profitable. Ells supported entrepreneurship in the region and urged the federal government to supply private sector investment. On his advice, the federal government invested in a drilling program to produce samples for further testing.

Ells theorized about "in situ" (meaning "in place"; going underground to seize the resource, rather than surface mining) operations as early as 1920 and produced a plan in 1936. It called for jetting water through tunnels and crosscuts. Technical questions led Ells to set aside the idea in the 1940s. Today, both heavy oil and oil sands projects apply in-situ steam injection.

Also to his credit, Ells was one of the first to publicly point out the importance of the oil sands to Canada's energy needs, and he cringed over any dispute between Alberta and the federal government. Max Ball, the American businessman behind the infamous and failed Abasand oil sands project, said in 1950: "S.C. Ells may well be called the father of the Alberta bituminous sand research and development. He made the first systematic study of the deposits and the first—and as yet the only—comprehensive maps of the area in which they lie. He made the first systematic study of methods for separating the bitumen from the sands. He first developed and demonstrated the principal of hot-water separation through pulping the bituminous sands and recovering the separated bitumen in a flotation cell. For 35 years, in the face of indifference and scepticism, he has been the courageous and unremitting advocate of the value and importance of the bituminous sand deposits."

In October 1945, investigating at Steepbank, Ells, then in his 60s, spent most of three days standing ankle-deep in cold water, which brought on a "severe attack of sciatica" (nerve pain in the hips and thighs). He spent five sleepless nights at a McMurray hotel, where he was helped by a friendly bartender, and wound up in hospital in Edmonton. A month later, in November 1945, his pension came through and Ells retired.

Ells knew that eventually the oil sands would become a major industry in Canada. He pointed out that in 1912,

Canada imported 93 percent of its petroleum needs at a cost of $89 million. After 1946, that cost would have risen to more than $500 million had it not been for discoveries in Western Canada, he said. "The impact of such a situation on our balance of trade requires no comment," wrote Ells.

His determination had some payoff. He attended the 1967 grand opening ceremonies at Great Canadian Oil Sands and even served as an adviser to that first major commercial project. He died in Victoria in 1971 at the age of 92.

Ells spent his life developing a love for the wilderness while he investigated the potential of the oil sands. Looking back, he wrote: "In biting cold of northern winters and sultry heat of summer days, to have had a part however small in the stirring saga of the awakening North has been adequate reward."

Ells' prodding about in Athabasca led to the discovery of several preserved, ancient wood specimens, some millions of years old. He submitted samples to Harvard University and learned that the genus was unlike any that currently exist in North America.

Bitumania

A standard barrel of oil contains 158.9 litres, based on the historical reference of 19th-century wooden barrels.

Crude oil is processed into a variety of products. About 65 percent of original volume is converted into gasoline and diesel. Light and heavy fuel oils, used for home heating and electric power generation, account for 15 percent. Aviation fuel accounts for another seven percent, while the refining process itself utilizes about five percent. The remainder is made into numerous items including asphalt, lubricants, wax and polish and as the basis for polystyrene and synthetic rubber.

CHAPTER SEVEN

Karl Clark
A Federal Scientist Becomes the Province's
Lead Oil Sands Investigator

IT IS A FITTING TRIBUTE THAT ONE OF THE ROADS WINDING THROUGH the Edmonton Research Park is named after Karl Clark. The park is dedicated to enabling and enhancing development of the city's and Alberta's technology companies. Few scientists have as much historical significance to Alberta as Clark, who is credited with early developments that led to effective oil sands processing later applied by the likes of Syncrude and Suncor.

Clark's story begins with an enquiry to Ottawa in 1913, when the Jean Cote letter representing a group of Edmonton businessmen, educators and city officials asked the federal government what information it had about the Athabasca tar sands. The Mines Branch realized that information was lacking. Sidney Ells of the department was dispatched to the rugged Athabasca territory to investigate and produced a report. Before releasing it, the Mines Branch asked two junior scientists, Karl Clark and Joseph Keele, to assess the material. Both were critical of the work, but realized that the oil sands held promise.

Toronto-born Clark visited the prairies in 1918 and noticed that the clay roads were rendered almost useless by rain. He wondered if the oil sands could provide material to waterproof roadbeds. Laboratory work using soap provided a bit of a surprise. Instead of producing a consistent mixture, the process separated the sand and oil. Clark experimented with a variety of soaps, and the results were consistent: the sand sank in his beaker, while the oils settled on top of the soap and the water on top of the oil.

Meanwhile, as federal interest in the oil sands waned, Dr. Marshall Tory of the University of Alberta refused to give up. Tory, son of a Nova Scotia farmer, was trained as a Methodist minister at McGill University in Montréal, but switched to mathematics and science. The U of A was established in 1908 with Tory as its first president, dedicated to building a post-secondary institution that served the needs of all Albertans. He travelled throughout the province encouraging people to consider university. Part of his commitment to the province included developing a base of expertise on the province's resource wealth.

Tory didn't like the federal policy regarding the oil sands, which had switched from direct government involvement to the promotion of private endeavour. The U of A president's view was that the resource belonged to Albertans, so giving over development to the private sector risked too much loss to the public good. Tory assigned U of A chemistry professor Adolph Lehmann to study the oil sands. Lehmann's research began with the chemical composition of the sandy bitumen, and during the World War I years, he tested the material to see if it could be used for explosives. Lehmann also began to look at separation methods.

While Lehmann was busy in the laboratory, Tory began gathering all available oil sands data, including a request to Ottawa for Ells' report. The Ells document arrived along with the Clark and Keele criticism. Echoing Clark and Keele, Lehmann gave Tory a similar assessment of Ells' work. In Tory's plans, Ells had been a potential researcher for the new university, but the bad reviews on his report created doubt. After the war, Ells applied for government funding to visit oil shales in Scotland. Tory was willing to kick in some money, but demanded a written report to the Legislature to outline the findings. Typically, Ells was reluctant to reveal the information, and Tory's assessment of the young scientist fell further. Already at this early stage, animosity was brewing between the province and the federal government over control and development of Alberta's resources. There was consideration for combined federal and provincial research, but it soon became apparent that the two governments were on different tracks. The federal government wanted to position Ells at the university under its control, while Tory insisted that any work at the U of A was under its jurisdiction. Tory would have to find someone else to lead oil sands research.

In addition, a 1920 study at McGill found that the oil sands would only provide road paving material and little else. That simply didn't match the research at the U of A, where the belief was that the oil sands had a much wider application, including petroleum oils. Soon, Lehmann was having trouble obtaining federal grants for oil sands separation research.

It was clear Alberta was on its own and needed a research institute into tar sands and the province's other abundant carbon resource, coal. While inquiring about suitable staff, Tory's attention turned to Clark.

The U of A and the provincial government formed the Scientific and Industrial Research Council, which would, in 1981, become the Alberta Research Council (the council's address today is 250 Karl Clark Road in Edmonton). In 1920, Tory offered Clark, who had completed a successful experiment separating oil from tar sand using a chemical additive, the position of research professor, with the mandate of using "fresh eyes" to improve the process.

Questioning whether it was possible to stabilize prairie dirt roads by bitumen treatment so they could better withstand wet or cold weather, Clark wrote in 1921 that the northern Alberta tar sands came to mind. Why not, he asked, emulsify the "asphaltic bituminous" that they contained? His 1920–21 budget amounted to $300.

Clark's appointment intensified a clash with Ells, who was convinced he was the better researcher on the subject. Historians find some truth in Ells' argument that he was first on the right path about the oil sands, but also note that his research was sloppy and ill defined. In addition, Tory assigned Clark to start from scratch. It was Clark who systematically provided the groundwork for future commercial oil sands operations, which are today a multi-billion-dollar effort. Once Clark took up the post, the riddle of the oil sands became his life's work. "Once the tar sticks to your boots, you can never get it off," he said.

The new provincial investigator set out to determine how well the tar sand could be used as a road surface material, and secondly, how best to separate the oil. In a memo to Tory in late 1921, Clark set out his work program, with six major initiatives. They included setting up a small demonstration separation plant, securing data on operations (quantity of reagents, temperatures, time factors, yields) and testing whether refined tar sands product could be used in business applications such as road surfacing or glassmaking.

Within a year, Clark reported to Tory: "Something definite has been accomplished and a very considerable glimmer of daylight let through the problem." Later, he urged that a next step in tar sands investigation must be small-scale development on the type and arrangement of a commercial-sized operation plant. To enable Clark's research, the U of A hauled in six tonnes of oil sand from Athabasca and dumped it next to his laboratory on campus.

By 1923, Clark and his assistant Sydney Blair, an engineer, had developed a hot-water system that extracted oil from small batches of sands. Raw bitumen was fed into two rotating drums and combined with hot water and steam. The mix created a froth that allowed oil to be skimmed from the surface, while the sand grains sank away. The pair built the prototype in a basement office of the U of A power plant building. That, in turn, led to the construction of a larger plant at the Dunvegan railyards, which were then on the city's outskirts.

Blair and Clark became close friends, sharing a pleasure for exploring in the forests and canoeing wild rivers. During a 1925 field journey with Blair, Clark recalled paddling far downstream to Fort Chipewyan, where they planned to get on board a steamer for transport back up the fast current to McMurray. The steamer arrived the day they reached Chipewyan, but was going downriver rather than up, so they took the opportunity, got on and saw some more of the northern province before the boat turned upstream again. Clark wrote that the detour offered no loss of time or expense.

Blair, after earning a master's degree in mining engineering at the U of A, left in 1926 and went on to a good career as an international oil consultant. However, he wasn't done with the Alberta oil sands and would emerge again in 1951. Also in 1926, Clark toured U.S. and Ontario refineries and found little interest in Alberta's oil sands, though he was encouraged to continue his work.

In 1927, the research council released "Report No. 18, The Bituminous Sands of Alberta," the first document from Clark. The report again promoted oil sands as road asphalt, but also admitted that the cost of transporting material from Athabasca was a limiting factor in any future plans for market-sized output.

Clark bemoaned the fact that no researcher alone had enough funding to accomplish anything. Bickering continued between the province and Ottawa over the jurisdiction of resources. A truce was reached in 1929, but it was short-lived. At that time, Alberta's research council and the federal Mines Branch formed a two-year agreement to run a "Bituminous Sands Advisory Committee." At about the same time, Clark's project was ready to move towards a prototype plant. He began to search for a suitable site to launch a pilot project based on a $30,000 allocation from the research council. That same year, Clark learned that Ells had secured $50,000 in federal funding for a pilot of his own. (Budgeting was always an issue at the Alberta council. Its 1923 allocation was $36,000, including $16,000 for salaries from a provincial budget of $9 million. By 1930, its budget was $85,000, including $45,000 for operations and the rest for payroll, from a $15 million provincial budget. Clark's salary was comfortable for the time—$4000 in 1930.)

After modifying the Dunvegan plant, Clark then dismantled it so it could be shipped by rail and barge to a site on the Clearwater River near McMurray. It was set it up by October 29, 1929, and managed to produce 11 barrels of bitumen in three days, but the water content of the finished product was higher than what Clark's lab experiments had predicted. His crew was back in the spring to try again, battling mechanical problems with the plant plus variances in the oil sands. But as the summer went on, the plant produced 60,000 litres of oil at a better consistency than in the lab. Clark was pleased—most of the frustrations were mechanical or related to the consistency of the bitumen, while the basic separation process seemed to be working. Product from the Clearwater plant was used to pave Edmonton roads.

In the 1930 research council annual report, Clark stated, "a separation plant has been built and successfully operated in the north country at the deposits. This had psychological as well as technical values."

First, the federal government transferred natural resources rights to the provinces in 1930 (but it didn't become clear until later that a caveat maintained Ottawa's grip on 5180 square kilometres, including some of the Athabasca oil sands). Secondly, American businessman Max Ball began making the rounds in Ottawa and Edmonton to shore up details on a proposed operation that later became the troubled Abasand project.

Unfortunately, the Depression set in and council funding dried up. Clark retreated to Chicago but returned in 1942 after funding resumed. Now, the intent was to move the separation process into a commercial scale. After the war, the province considered the oil sands as an opportunity to broaden the economy and increase energy supply. However, Alberta's conventional oilfield drilling surged with the Leduc discovery in 1947—a strike so massive that it encouraged further exploration and more discoveries. The conventional oil boom made oil sands an even tougher sell when it came to funding and research.

The full potential of the oil sands could not be reached without private sector investment—the government simply couldn't go it alone, Clark now realized. A number of oil sands operations started up. Sometimes Clark was ignored; sometimes he gave advice. All the new plants failed, but mostly for business or political reasons—there was nothing basically wrong with the separation process. However, it wasn't until after his lengthy career had ended that the first successful, large-scale production venture, Great Canadian Oil Sands (GCOS), was launched.

Clark retired in 1954 but continued working indirectly on oil sands development as an adviser to graduate students and to GCOS—the precursor to Suncor. He was on hand for the GCOS sod turning in 1965 but died nine months before its 1967 opening.

Bitumania

Although he had spent his career trying to determine the best way to conquer the oil sands, Karl Clark was deeply saddened by the damage to the Athabasca countryside caused by the massive strip mining operations. Shortly before his death from cancer, he told his daughter Mary that he didn't want to ever return to the area.

Children on Clark Crescent in Fort McMurray attend Karl A. Clark School.

CHAPTER EIGHT

Regulating Oil and Gas
Turner Valley Flaring Raises
a Burning Issue

THE FLARING AT TURNER VALLEY ESTABLISHED A NEED FOR BETTER OIL and gas regulation in Alberta. After Dingman No. 1, flaring caused minor criticism but no large complaint. That changed to an outcry after Royalite No. 4 blew out in 1924. An estimated six million cubic metres of natural gas burned each day—the equivalent of about 22,675 tonnes of coal per day.

Regulation of Western Canada's natural resources began shortly after the July 1870 surrender of Rupert's Land (Manitoba and parts of Alberta, Saskatchewan and the Northwest Territories) to the federal government. From 1873 to 1930, the federal Department of the Interior administered mineral resources. Rules governing mineral exploitation were tinkered with until 1887, when a significant change took place—the Crown separated surface and mineral rights, with the latter reserved to Her Majesty. The rule applied to all companies except those that were active in the area prior to the change: the Hudson's Bay Company and rail lines, including Canadian Pacific Railway. In 1890, another amendment gave specific recognition to petroleum exploration as opposed to coal or other minerals. Under the new rule, an applicant had to swear an affidavit explaining his belief that petroleum existed below the site. That location was then reserved for five years, and the government would only sell to the applicant once a producing well had been proved. By 1898, Dominion regulations allowed the reservation of land in southern Alberta of 640 acres for six months; if oil was found, the reserved land could be bought at $1 per acre plus 2.25 percent on all sales. In 1901, the government allowed a $3 per acre charge over the original 640 acres, up to a maximum of 1920 acres. By 1906, rules were also in place for natural gas production.

Then, in 1910, another important change took place when the federal government abandoned the sale of rights in favour of leases, which were available for 21 years at 25 cents per acre the first year and 50 cents per acre in advance each year after. A 21-year renewal was also available. Companies could credit some expenses against lease charges. Boring had to begin within 15 months of the start of the lease. Bill Herron was among the first applicants to take leases under the 1910 provisions, and those were at Turner Valley.

Regulations for petroleum and natural gas were combined in 1914, and these regulations contained a prohibition against the unnecessary waste of gas and requirements for the proper closing of wells—the first conservation laws governing natural resources.

The federal government changed its royalty structure for petroleum in 1919. No royalty was charged for five years after discovery, then 2.5 percent to five percent was charged on sales during the next five years, five percent to 10 percent for the following five years and finally 10 percent for the remaining life of the well.

By 1921, an auction process was in place for leases cancelled because of royalty arrears or missed drilling deadlines.

For its part, the province passed the Oil and Gas Wells Act in 1926, but it was hardly enforced and was easily ignored since the federal government was in charge of natural resources. The Alberta legislation covered all land except HBC holdings, rail reserves and homesteads established before 1887 and was intended to prevent waste. It gave the province authority over all aspects of oil and gas, including well location, takeover of dangerous wells and production restrictions.

Then everything changed in 1930, when the federal government transferred natural resources control to the provinces. When Alberta was created in 1905, the province was granted a yearly subsidy in place of oil and gas revenues. By 1910, the province was negotiating with Ottawa to gain control of its own resource base. More than 19,000 federal leases were in place when Alberta took over control of the industry in 1930. Historian Aubrey Kerr, an Imperial Oil Leduc 1947 veteran, has suggested that the transfer is the most important event in Alberta's history and accounts for the province's current prosperity.

At the time of the transfer, Royalite No. 4 had already been in production for six years, and the flaring at Hell's Half Acre lit up the night sky, annoying Calgarians, who were paying high rates on short supply of natural gas. And Turner Valley wasn't the only place in Alberta where conservationists saw waste. There seemed to be a belief that the earth produced natural gas as fast as it was drawn out—an erroneous assumption that provided tough lessons first learned at depleting wells in the United States. Conservationist Frank Adams of McGill University, chairman of the federal Commission of Conservation's Committee on Minerals, pointed to Medicine Hat as a symbol of waste.

"The inevitable tendency of this, as seen in Medicine Hat at the present time, is to allow the gas in the street lamps to burn all day, seeing that it costs no more to do so, while at the same time it is easier to let it burn than to turn it out, and the spectacle of gas blazing throughout the day conveys a general suggestion of the abundance of a product that one can afford to waste so lavishly," Adams stated.

It was under these circumstances that Premier John Brownlee, together with the United Farmers of Alberta (UFA), requested that industry comply voluntarily with provincial conservation rules, but was rebuffed. Flaring continued unabated. At a meeting in Edmonton, industry representatives suggested that any enforced production cutback would amount to a confiscation of property. Bill Herron stepped up to suggest that a group was prepared to build a pipeline to Montana that would carry 12 million cubic metres of gas per day, a move that would solve the flaring problem completely. But the idea of selling Albertans short of gas was less palatable than flaring.

With no indication from industry that voluntary action would be taken, the province toughened up its legislation and enforcement. The 1931 Oil and Gas Wells Act update required producers to put up a $10,000 bond before drilling could begin—to ensure that regulations were followed—and to conduct mandatory pressure testing. The province also ordered a 40 percent cutback in production at every well, and was ignored. Brownlee then ordered an 80 percent cut, enraging producers. Herron likened the move to communism. He complained that if the UFA government could confiscate the property of people who invested in oil, then farmers should "have no complaint if the communists demand that they give up the farms for the benefit of those who have none."

Mary Gillanders, a member of the Associated Women Shareholders of Turner Valley Oil and Gas, also complained to the legislature and said they were prepared to fight. "Many poor men and women have placed their all in this venture. Are you, members of this house who have enforced this conservation, prepared to reimburse these people for their loss?"

Another series of meetings between government and industry was fruitless, with one at the Legislature ending in a hallway fist fight. The province turned again to legislation, this time bringing in the Turner Valley Gas Conservation Act, which established a three-man conservation board and set out a reduction in output of six million cubic metres per day. Spooner Oils successfully fought the board in court, winning a ruling that Alberta law could not apply to natural resource development that had been initiated prior to the 1930 turnover of federal leases to provincial control. As a result, the board was disbanded.

In 1935, Alberta shifted again when voters brought in Premier William Aberhart and a new Social Credit regime that would last for 36 years. Aberhart's vision included a dividend payment to every Albertan, based on the prosperity of the province. (Aberhart would be the first of three Alberta premiers to dole out prosperity cheques.) The province had plenty of land, farms, food, lumber, coal—everything people needed to work, produce and keep an economy going.

"What greater bondage could there be than to see people starve or suffer unnecessary privation in the midst of abundant plenty?" asked Aberhart.

Under the plan, the Social Credit government would give each Albertan $25 a month financed on the province's "credit." Unfortunately, the province didn't have much credit—in fact, it hardly had enough to meet payroll. In addition, the idea of free money didn't stimulate economic growth, but rather promoted freeloading. Men quit their jobs in expectation of a steady provincial dividend, and others rolled in on trains asking for the dividend office. There was a small boom in holiday reservations. Eventually, the Socred's dividend experiment failed. Aberhart appointed Charles Ross, a former federal mines inspector in Calgary, as the new provincial minister of lands and mines. Ross tried to bring in quotas at Turner Valley but was overruled by Aberhart. At a meeting with a producer in Black Diamond, Ross complained that since 1912, there had been "$104 million worth of gas wasted to produce $23 million worth of oil." The lands and mines minister then moved to shut down some of the most damaging Turner Valley wells. Soon, Ross was gone. Officially, he resigned over a dispute about another cabinet appointment, but Ross later said he had been fired.

Youthful and good-looking Nathan Tanner, who would hold the job for 18 years, replaced him. Tanner ran smack into the same problem as those before him—nobody in industry was about to comply with voluntary cutbacks or other measures to control flaring or output. Aberhart blamed the federal government—always good politics in Alberta. Thus in 1937, Ottawa and Alberta agreed to amend the 1929 deal.

At last, in 1938, a new Oil and Gas Conservation Act was passed, creating in turn the Petroleum and Natural Gas Conservation Board, precursor of today's Alberta Energy and Utilities Board (EUB). But fighting between the province and Ottawa—the feds battled Aberhart's controversial monetary policies in court—delayed federal ratification of the new provincial system.

The act applied to all lands this time, with no exceptions for former federal or freehold leases. It gave the province the right to prevent the exhaustion of a producing area and to pro-ration (divide) output in high-activity areas such as Turner Valley. Once a discovery was made, the energy company was required to map out its lease in blocks as on a checkerboard. The company paid for half the blocks, while the rest reverted to the province, which could auction off the rights. The checkerboard system allowed smaller or more cautious producers a chance to get in on the action, but the blocks were of sufficient size to prevent fly-by-night outfits from shooting in and siphoning off the reservoir that someone else had found. The new energy board had power of inquiry similar to the courts and took evidence under oath. Failure to comply with a board order could result in a summary conviction carrying a fine of up to $2000 plus costs and $500 per day for continuing default. No staff or member of the board could be held personally responsible for acts carried out under its mandate.

The act was based on conservation experiences in the U.S. There was also some change in industry attitude because of a growing understanding of how energy reservoirs acted. Companies had come to realize that excess gas production could reduce underground pressure, making oil recovery difficult, whereas conserving natural gas could prolong oil production. A new crude oil discovery in Turner Valley suddenly created an industry need for gas conservation.

Bill Knode, the first chairman of the new Conservation Board, was a Texan with a track record in his home state of winning over oil companies to voluntary controls. Knode was used to wrangling with big-time business and wasn't the type to be easily pushed around. He instantly became the highest-paid provincial employee at $1000 per month plus $8 per day for expenses, double a provincial cabinet minister's pay. Calgary was named as the board's headquarters, a move that confirmed the city as the province's energy capital.

As production at Turner Valley heightened, Aberhart was forced to make a humble plea to Prime Minister Mackenzie King. The federal enabling legislation passed in June 1938.

Knode made it clear that waste would not be tolerated. Production would be linked to market demand and no more. The board's first directive came out in August, ordering appropriate well spacing at Turner Valley. In addition, all future applications would be subject to a hearing—EUB hearings today provide an important public input platform on development. Production was prohibited at any well that didn't have a ready market for its gas. In late August, the board announced its pro-rationing schedule for Turner Valley, which met with general approval from crude operators and grumbling from the gas guys. A small group complained that its production would be curtailed to the benefit of large players in the Alberta market, such as Imperial Oil.

It wasn't long before the board's orders regarding Turner Valley were challenged in court. Historian David Breen reports a "nose-to-nose" confrontation between Knode and Mercury Oils president Albert Mayland, during which Knode said that company wells would be sealed with valves, and if Mercury broke the seals, Mayland would be thrown in jail. Mercury's court application was thrown out on a legal procedural issue, but not before the board took a beating. Because it seemed like a heated court battle was brewing, the Aberhart government toughened the Oil and Gas Conservation Act to make board actions firm.

On September 14, 1938, the Turner Valley flares were extinguished.

Bitumania

The "law of capture" suggests that the owner of a well is entitled to everything it could produce, even if the well drew from a reservoir that spread out under someone else's lease. This legal concept stood well into the 1950s in Alberta. Accordingly, if you had a lease, it was best to get going on it before someone drilled next door and sucked up all your oil or gas.

CHAPTER NINE

The Browns
A Calgary Father-and-Son Team Drills Deep and Goes Big

MOST OPERATORS HAD COME TO ACCEPT THAT TURNER VALLEY WAS a rich gas field and would not produce oil. They were wrong.

A father-and-son team of Robert Brown, senior and junior, became one of the most successful wildcat operators in Alberta and made a fortune by trying something that hadn't been done at Turner Valley—drilling deep for oil.

Brown Sr. was superintendent of the City of Calgary's Light and Power Department, which ran the electric lights and streetcar system, earning him the nickname "Streetcar." But he also had an interest in private business, particularly oil. The door to his Calgary office carried a list of companies in which he had invested.

Ever since Dingman No. 1, Brown Sr. believed there was oil under all that Turner Valley gas. So in 1934, he partnered with George Bell, owner of the *Albertan* newspaper, and Calgary lawyer John Moyer to form Turner Valley Royalties Ltd. Their theory was that the Turner Valley deposit was on an angle, with the gas sitting on top under high pressure, and the oil hiding deep at the lower end to the southwest. This was contrary to geological understanding of the time. According to Streetcar Brown, reaching the oil would require drilling the deepest—and accordingly most expensive—well in Canada to that point.

Because it was the Depression and Turner Valley was in one of its low ebbs in terms of production and new discovery, financing was hard to find. The new company was forced to commit 70 percent of production to royalty payments, hence the company's name. They set up a trust and sold one percent royalty units at $1500 each. By April 1934, enough financing was in place to spud the well, but they were forced to stop drilling seven times when the money ran out. Brown mortgaged his house, sold his car and borrowed against his life insurance.

Bell was already deeply in debt. His newspapers weren't doing well, and he'd invested heavily in earlier unsuccessful oil ventures. Bell was Turner Valley Royalties' first president, but he didn't live to see the first well completed. He died in March 1936, leaving his son Max Bell the *Albertan* and $500,000 debt. Max Bell took his inheritance and went on to create great wealth in both oil and publishing.

The desperate company kept selling royalties. Imperial Oil pitched in $22,500 worth of equipment for a 7.5 percent royalty. British American Oil loaned $30,000, while companies such as Spooner Oils and Calmont Oils each bought five percent royalties for $7500.

About three months after Bell's death, Brown visited his troubled well. The crew had begun with a cable-tool rig, which painfully, slowly, ground down about 914 metres. At that point, it was replaced with a more modern rotary rig with a diamond bit, which picked up the pace of drilling. On June 16, Brown observed bits of oil in the drilling mixture and ordered the mud pumped out. As the mud gurgled out, crude oil gushed, then erupted with a roar high over the rig. Turner Valley Royalties had proven Brown's theory at 2081 metres, the deepest well so far. Oil rained down on the crew, and Brown revelled in it.

"He practically took a bath in it with his clothes on," said rig hand Fin Lineham, who was also later at Leduc No. 1. "Standing in there with oil all over 'im. He knew he had it made." The *Calgary Herald* reported that it was the first crude oil gusher in Canada.

The strike enticed drillers to spud hundreds of deep wells in the vicinity, and Turner Valley became the largest oilfield in the British Empire. No other significant find was made until 11 years later at Leduc. During World War II, even the federal government got in on it, establishing Wartime Oils Ltd. to finance more drilling at Turner Valley, to produce more oil needed to fuel the war effort. One of Wartime Oils' biggest contractors was Bill Herron's Okalta. By mid-war, Turner Valley had 232 oil wells producing 28,410 barrels per day.

Turner Valley Royalties No. 1 initially drew 850 barrels of oil and 60,000 cubic metres of gas per day. Brown Jr. was a 21-year-old student studying commerce at the University of Alberta when his father's Turner Valley gusher came in. Brown Jr. quit school, while his father resigned from the City of Calgary, and together they set off, using the new revenue to fund more oil exploration. Soon they had a series of wells on the leases near the first strike.

The Browns then went through a period of dry holes, but their enthusiasm rekindled when Imperial Oil made its discovery in 1947 at Leduc. But Brown Sr. wouldn't live to see the next big development: he died in 1948 at 62 of a heart attack stemming from years of alcoholism and anemia. Brown Jr., known as Bobby, took charge.

Unfortunately, he shared his father's penchant for booze. Nevertheless, the Brown's were respected members of the Canadian oil patch, known for their personal integrity. A well-known photograph of both men shows Brown Sr. sitting, double-chinned and bespectacled, with Bobby standing at his right, youthful and wavy-haired. Both are in tidy ties and jackets.

Bobby had spent the last two years of the war as a petroleum procurement officer for the navy in Ottawa. Buying oil wasn't all he was after. In his spare time, Bobby found alcohol, a somewhat rare wartime commodity, and used it to develop government contacts. After the war, he spent a few years importing U.S. radios and washing machines before a government crackdown on luxury imports because of a currency crisis.

After his father's death, Bobby took over Federated Petroleums, the consolidated Brown oil company with 17 wells at Turner Valley, which were quickly depleting. Looking for corporate renewal, Bobby became one of the biggest debtors in the Canadian oil patch. He borrowed from the Bank of Commerce: $4.35 million to buy Frank McMahon's and Imperial Oil's Turner Valley operations (other than Royalite), $8 million to buy open market shares of Home Oil (eventually amounting to 25 percent of the outstanding shares), $3.25 million for Home Oil to acquire Federated (and give Bobby control of both) and a significant part of $30 million to buy up shares of Trans-Canada Pipelines. Bobby built himself up into one of the biggest independent operators in the Canadian oil patch.

"I have an effective arrangement with my managers," said Bobby. "I find the money, and they find the oil."

Home Oil became one of the most successful wildcatting operations Canada had ever seen. Its biggest success came at Swan Hills in 1957, at the time the second largest find in the country. From 1954 to 1960, the company's reserves increased by six times.

Yet at the same time, Home Oil's rate of production was falling, as were sales revenues. In an effort to broaden markets for Alberta oil, Brown became part of a group that lobbied the federal government to push a pipeline through from Alberta direct to Montréal, the nation's largest petroleum refining centre. But Québec was paying bargain prices for imported crude oil. A pipeline from Alberta would require a federal embargo on foreign imports, a move that was likely to increase Québec prices. One study suggested that Alberta-pipelined oil would cost Québecers 10 percent more than imported product.

The world situation didn't help Alberta. Oil was a worldwide commodity, and there was lots of it. Demand for Alberta oil fell, and the U.S. even applied voluntary quotas in an effort to protect domestic operators.

The Borden Commission, set up to investigate energy issues, held a hearing in Calgary in 1958, at which Brown noted that in 1956, Canada imported 230,000 barrels per day when Alberta had idle production of 430,000 barrels a day. The commission made no specific finding on the pipeline, but suggested that Canadian crude was at a competitive disadvantage to imported petroleum (oil is a lot cheaper to find and extract in some parts of the world). It suggested that enforced movement of Canadian crude to Montréal would "result in either a reduction of wellhead prices to the producer in Western Canada or higher prices for refined petroleum products to the consumer in Eastern Canada—quite possibly a combination of both."

The commission recommended a national energy policy controlled by a governing board. The Borden recommendations resulted in a national energy system with two spheres: Québec and the east with imported crude, and the rest primarily fed from Alberta.

By 1968, Home Oil had $11 million in net earnings on $26 million revenues. Bobby Brown worked out of the Home Oil building, which was decorated in ebony, rosewood, walnut and lava rock from all over the world. He travelled in a private Gulfstream jet with dolphin-shaped taps in the bathroom. The ostentatious appearances were part of Bobby's strategy to suggest to borrowers that he really didn't need the money. But eventually, he did.

His alcoholism, reminiscent of his father, was a growing problem, and Bobby inevitably hit a losing streak on his characteristic oil gambling. In 1969, he bet vast sums— some Home Oil money, some his own—on the Prudhoe Bay play in Alaska. It was a huge flop. Home Oil shares trading at $80 each in 1969 fell to $20 in 1971. In a bid to recover, Home Oil bet on the Alaskan North Slope, again to failure.

By 1970, Bobby had amassed a personal debt of $26 million, had three heart attacks and a stroke. After a failed attempt to sell Home Oil to a U.S. buyer, he sold controlling interest to Consumers' Gas of Toronto to stave off bankruptcy. He died of a fourth heart attack at the age of 57 in January 1972.

Bitumania

The first oil drilling rigs were wooden towers strung through with cables and could penetrate about 100 metres per month. Today's sophisticated rigs can drill that deep in a matter of hours. The deepest well drilled in Alberta was 5500 metres.

Mud, made up of a wide variation of water, clay and chemicals, is the name of the stuff that rig hands send down the hole to lubricate and cool the bit, remove rock cuttings and control pressure. Get the mud consistency wrong and you could have a blowout. That's why making and selling downhole products such as mud is big business.

CHAPTER TEN

Bitumount
Robert Fitzsimmons' Plant Ends
under Provincial Control

IN THE EARLY 1900S, MCMURRAY WAS A REMOTE OUTPOST, AND the pioneers of oil sands development were adventurers, scientists, risk-takers, obsessives and, in some cases, frauds. After Karl Clark's initial research endeavour, commercial production got off to a rough start.

Imperial Oil sent a geologist to the oil sands in 1914, and he estimated the total resource at 30 billion barrels. Accordingly, Imperial Oil subsidiary North West Company drilled two wells in 1917 and 1918, but found nothing to encourage further development. Despite that, Imperial Oil is today a large shareholder in the Syncrude oil sands consortium.

Oil equipment manufacturer Thomas Draper of Petrolia, Ontario, set up McMurray Asphaltum and Oil and made significant headway in using oil sands for road surfacing. He also supplied oil sands to other organizations, including Alberta's research council, but was disappointed by criticism from Clark. Draper also took a dislike to Sidney Ells, considering him arrogant, and once ordered him off the site. Draper did research of his own, setting up a $35,000 plant near Fort McMurray, which was destroyed by fire in 1924. He showed his paving process at the Edmonton Exhibition and even paved part of Wellington Street and Parliament Hill in Ottawa under a federal contract. Most of Draper's paving work was in Alberta, including 22 blocks of sidewalk in Camrose. But the McMurray operation was plagued with problems and had trouble meeting federal lease requirements. Draper shut it down in 1936 and headed back east.

A couple of companies, one out of Calgary and another whose principal officer was from Montana, attempted steam injection into well bores, again without much success. From the sidelines, Ells and Clark observed them all, sometimes bemused, sometimes wary.

Robert Fitzsimmons, originally from Prince Edward Island, was determined to make his fortune in the heavy oil deposits of northern Alberta. He established one of the first working oil sands plants at a place he named Bitumount (basically a postal address that Fitzsimmons got approved in 1937), about 90 kilometres north of McMurray. Historians believe that Bitumount marked a critical point in oil sands development because it was the first commercial operation, and it improved the separation process.

Initially a farmer before he went into real estate in Washington State, Fitzsimmons moved to Alberta in 1922. In 1925, he took over the Alcan Oil Company, an exploration outfit formed by some New York policemen, which had been drilling around the Bitumount site. He reorganized the company into the International Bitumen Co., and then he went on a relentless drilling campaign around Bitumount. Throughout the 1920s, Fitzsimmons made regular claims that he'd hit pools of bitumen, but experts realized that he was misinterpreting small bits of oil that separated in the heat caused by the drilling process.

Discouraged by lack of success with conventional drilling, Fitzsimmons set up a hot-water separation plant in

June 1930. Oil sand was shovelled into a tank, where it mixed with hot water before being siphoned to a second tank, where the bitumen was skimmed by hand. The operation was similar to Clark's experimental plant, and though Fitzsimmons claimed he came up with it himself, it was built after he had seen Clark's outfit on the Clearwater River. Fitzsimmons' seven-man crew produced about 300 barrels of crude oil bitumen in its first two months. The crude was shipped first by river barge, then rail to Edmonton. The product was sold for roof waterproofing, but International Bitumen also advertised that the sticky goo could be used in fuels, lubrication oils, printers' ink, medicines, rust- and acid-proofing paints, fireproof roofing, street paving, patent leather and fence post preservatives. The company's sale pitch called bitumen "Nature's Supreme Gift to Industry."

Further success came in 1931, with a rebuilt plant that included a boiler. Fitzsimmons spent a small fortune, especially for those days, of about $200,000 on two years of operation. The new operation impressed Clark. Encouraged, Fitzsimmons went looking for both buyers and more investors, unshakeable in his determination. But with the Depression building, there were few takers. Notably, he shipped some bitumen samples to U.S. businessman Max Ball, who would be the main organizer and operator of the Abasand project. Ball used the samples in laboratory tests at Denver and Toronto.

During a U.S. tour to promote his plant and product, Fitzsimmons met Harry Everard, a petroleum engineer, in Los Angeles. Everard was hired, but only after he was convinced of the potential at Bitumount, including that a ready market was available upriver where mining operators needed fuel. Consolidated Mining and Smelting (CM&S)

had operations at Lake Athabasca and Great Bear Lake. Proximity would give Bitumount an advantage over suppliers father south. Selling to nearby CM&S was a strategy already applied by Ball at Abasand, which was by then up and running as a competitor to Bitumount. Everard was assigned to build a refinery at Bitumount and improve the separation plant to create capacity for the production of 635 tonnes per day of diesel oil and asphalt. Immediately, Everard ran up against a series of problems, including high sand and water content that couldn't be refined and a serious lack of funding to address the issues. By 1937, he had managed a start-up, but at lower production than planned. Then the system sputtered and puffed through a series of breakdowns. The situation was worsened by the fact that employees weren't getting paid. The plant suspended operations in September, and a legal battle over wages ensued, with Fitzsimmons, vexed and bitter, going as far as accusing Everard of sabotage.

Everard was replaced with Elmer Adkins, a University of Alberta–trained engineer who cobbled things together and managed $3000 in sales to CM&S in 1938. Adkins resigned in September that year because he hadn't been paid either. By December, the last 16 staff, all unpaid, walked away. Tapped out, Fitzsimmons blamed saboteurs, bad employees, meddling government officials, large oil competitors—anyone but himself. He left for Chicago to avoid his debts.

In 1942, he sold International Bitumen to Lloyd Champion of Montréal, who renamed it Oil Sands Ltd. International Bitumen and the oil sands' first commercial separation and refining plant were finished. Sidney Ells, who had supported Bitumount despite Fitzsimmons' disdain, cited mismanagement and bad equipment for the failure.

By this point, Ball's Abasand plant was already in trouble of its own and was under federal control. Champion wasn't prepared to compete with government, so he struggled along, maintaining Bitumount and rebuilding systems while trying to find investors or a buyer. Defeated, he submitted a partnership proposal to the provincial government.

One of the province's goals was to promote development in the resource sector. In addition, the province was annoyed with the federal government over its involvement at Abasand. With the failure of both Bitumount and Abasand, the Social Credit government—averse to intervention by its doctrine—decided to take up Champion's offer and develop an experimental station. The province turned to its long-time expert Karl Clark for advice. Clark gave the nod to the experimental partnership with Champion, stressing that the separation process problems had to be tackled first before any commercial project could expect success. Any private endeavour would first want an idea of how much it had to spend and what it might get back.

"If the cost is not established soon, the resource may lie idle, needlessly, for years before some outside party appears," Clark warned. Realizing that private enterprise would not enter the oil sands until some promise of return had been displayed, the Ernest Manning government decided it had to be the catalyst.

Champion's proposal asked for a 10-year loan or loan guarantee with Oil Sands Ltd. maintaining commercial rights, and asked that the province handle material procurement. The province balked, seeing that the offer greatly benefited Oil Sands Ltd. compared to taxpayers, and demanded a direct partnership. By December 1944, they had a deal, and the province came up with $250,000 to get things moving. Elmer Adkins, the former Fitzsimmons' employee, was brought back as plant superintendent.

Surprisingly, the province then hired oil sands rookie Born Engineering of Tulsa, Oklahoma, to design the new Bitumount plant. When delays held up shipments in 1945, Clark wrote to Born Engineering to ensure they weren't under the belief that "roses bloom at Bitumount at Christmas just as at Tulsa." He also expressed concern about other operational aspects planned by Born Engineering.

Clark wasn't overly impressed with Champion either. Writing to old friend Sidney Blair, Clark coloured Champion as a good politician but "a washout so far as a good businessman is concerned."

Born Engineering was slow to produce, and it wasn't until summer 1947 that the new plant completed construction at double the original $250,000 budget. Clark estimated that another $250,000 would be required for fine-tuning before production. However, he liked what he saw. Again writing to his former colleague Sydney Blair, he compared the new Bitumount to Abasand: "We have a better plant, better equipment, all new, good instrumentation all on top of better tar sand to handle and right on the river 60 miles nearer the market and the cost will not exceed the $750,000 figure."

Soon Champion was hinting that Oil Sands Ltd. wanted out. By 1948, his company was unable to meet its required investment. The province was forced to take over completely. Later that year, Bitumount managed some limited production, but was hampered by low water levels in the river. Clark's misgivings about Born Engineering's plans for feeding sand into the plant and its skimmer also proved to be correct.

During a short period in June 1949, Bitumount under Adkins managed to produce 660 barrels per day. However, there were still problems with water intake, and Adkins advised the province that expensive upgrades were needed. Clark encouraged the province to press on.

Every plant to that point had produced at least a modest amount of oil, Clark noted. The big problem was that engineers had not found a way to run the hot-water process efficiently and without breakdown.

To this point, the province had spent about $1 million at Bitumount. Its September 1949 output was satisfactory. About that time, Blair visited Bitumount, and the province asked his opinion. On Blair's advice, the province agreed that Bitumount had served its purpose. A report prepared by Blair established that the oil sands could be profitable, but conceded it was unlikely to attract private investment when much cheaper conventional oil had been discovered elsewhere, such as Leduc. Blair estimated a working, efficient plant could cost $48 million. A third-party report suggested the cost would be more like $88 million. Faced with mounting upgrading costs to keep Bitumount going, the province instead bowed out.

Bitumount was then sold a few times, at one point merging with Abasand, before Royalite Oil Company closed operations in 1958. In 1974, Bitumount became a provincially designated historical site, though access is limited.

Bitumania

Petroleum is solid, liquid or gaseous hydrocarbons (carbon and hydrogen) and provides the base for oil, natural gas and coal.

Crude oil contains pentanes (hydrocarbons with five carbon atoms to 12 hydrogen) and heavier hydrocarbons (with more than five carbon atoms) and usually includes other substances such as water, natural gas, sulphur or other minerals. Conventional crude flows naturally or easily with pumping. Further, crude is classified as light, medium, heavy or extra heavy, referring to its specific gravity. Heavy oil is generally defined as that which can't be recovered just by drilling a hole or pumping. It needs a little extra push—sometimes a big push—to get moving.

Athabasca oil sands are a combination of sand, water, clay and crude. Each grain of sand is enveloped by water, and a film of bitumen surrounds the water. Oil content in the sands ranges from one percent to 20 percent. Once separated and refined, oil sands product becomes known as synthetic oil.

CHAPTER ELEVEN

Abasand
An American Businessman Tries
to Tackle the Oil Sands

SUCCESS IN THE OIL SANDS BEGINS WITH FAILURE. SEVERAL OF THEM. One of the biggest letdowns was the Abasand project on the Horse River. The story begins with federal scientist Sidney Ells and American businessman Max Ball.

In his 1962 information circular, Ells recalled: "I had selected in early June 1913, an area that might meet future requirements of paving material for western national parks. This area was to become known as the Horse River Reserve of the National Parks Branch; it included some 580 acres along the Horse River and was approximately one and a half miles from McMurray. The estimated tonnage available within the reserve was apparently large, while mining conditions were favourable and quality of material good." Ells' report, written long after Abasand's demise, seems understated: "This area subsequently proved to contain the only large workable deposit of sand within a reasonable distance of rail transportation. Consequently, during the period 1920–45, it became the scene of important activities and the principal focal point of attempts to develop a method for the recovery of bitumen on a commercial scale."

Ball had a background that included time as a field assistant with the U.S. Geological Survey. He had a degree in engineering and later got a law degree as well. Born in

1885, Ball was in business for himself by the 1920s. He first heard about a huge potential resource in Alberta from a friend who worked for a U.S. oil company with operations in Western Canada. Intrigued, Ball wrote to the Canadian federal government in 1929 requesting more information. The government passed Ball's request on to Ells.

The result was a meeting between Ball and Ells in Denver, Colorado. Jim McClave, a Ball colleague who would play a role in the extraction process applied at Abasand, also attended the meeting. McClave had already received samples from Athabasca and had done some lab testing. Ells suggested that McClave investigate warm-water separation and urged Ball and his associates to launch a company for the extraction of Athabasca sands. In 1930, McClave and Ball toured Athabasca, guided by Ells. Also relying on Alberta Research Council findings, Ball applied for oil sands leases, proposing to spend $150,000 for a commercial separation plant.

Ball initially launched Calgary-based Canadian Northern Oil Sands Production Ltd. in September that year, but the name was changed to Abasand Oils Ltd. in 1935. Ells could not afford to buy in, and besides, he had a conflict of interest as a government agent. However, Ball's entry into the oil sands at least provided some hope that Ells' belief in the oil sands would soon come true.

Although Canadian Northern Oil Sands launched at the beginning of the Depression, Ball still went out to markets looking for investment. He also released a statement to the press suggesting a plan to build a 10,000-barrel-a-day plant about 48 kilometres south of Waterways, the small rail terminus just south of McMurray; to connect the plant by pipeline to the railhead at Waterways; and to build a refinery at Edmonton. Ells lobbied Ottawa on behalf of Canadian Northern Oil Sands, and in 1930, Ball's company won a lease on 15 square kilometres beside the Horse River—Bituminous Sands Permit No. 1.

The Horse River lease set off more bickering between the provincial government and Ottawa. When the federal government transferred natural resources to the province in 1930, it quietly held back rights to the oil sands territory. Only weeks before the transfer was to take effect, Ottawa signed a lease with Ball, and the intrigue was revealed. Outraged, observers in Alberta worried that the federal government intended to develop the oil sands without provincial input. In addition, the feds had leased Ball one of the most promising sites in the oil sands, with an option for another 15 square kilometres anywhere in the deposit.

Ball also managed to obtain rights from the province, but with the condition he must build a 227-tonne-a-day plant. That year, he also paid $9200 to buy out the province's experimental Clearwater plant.

Back in Denver, McClave was working on a separation process. Still in need of investors, Ball ordered McClave to ship his experimental unit to Toronto for demonstration, but the show and tell garnered little interest. It took five more years of testing in the Denver lab and in Toronto before Ball was ready to begin construction on a commercial-scale plant. In terms of investment, he began to realize that he was mostly on his own. He moved his family to Edmonton in 1934 to get on with it.

In 1935, Ball took what little capital he and a few investors could scrape together, installed McClave as plant manager and launched the project. Observers credited Ball with being methodical and a good manager. By January 1936, a small area had been cleared at Horse River, and the oil sands project was under construction. Abasand Oils officially declared the plant open on September 1, 1936.

The first challenge to early optimism came when the oil sands around Horse River played tricks on the machinery. Hard sand wore out metal parts, then sand softened by summer heat stuck in the works. Finding the right method of extraction and separation turned out to be the biggest problem Abasand faced and never tackled. After trying several frustrating methods of bitumen removal, crews fell back on blasting as the best way to free up the precious resource. They loaded it into dump trucks and hauled it to the plant.

But Ball also made one important business move that Robert Fitzsimmons had initially missed at Bitumount—he found a big customer within easy distance. Ball was able to convince and contract Consolidated Mining and Smelting Co. (CM&S) of Trail, BC, which had major operations in the North. The mining company was impressed by a letter from Karl Clark, affirming the effectiveness of hot-water separation and suggesting the new plant could produce crude at about $1 per barrel, a good price. CM&S contracted for fuel oil supplies, and Ball had the final important link in the chain—a buyer.

In the interim, Ball turned to Ottawa looking for a waiver on royalties—a common source of complaint from developers as time went on.

By 1941, Abasand had processed 17,233 tonnes of sand to produce 17,000 barrels, which according to Ells were processed into gas, diesel, coke and fuel oil. Because of the high sulphur content, people in the region jokingly referred to the plant as "Abascent" or even "Skunk Hollow."

The production numbers were good, but Ottawa wanted output increased to 9070 tonnes per day.

Then disaster struck. On November 21, 1941, fire razed the Abasand separation unit. Damage was estimated at $250,000, a staggering blow, for although the company had been well managed, it had also been working on a tight budget. To that point, the few Abasand investors, primarily Ball, had spent about $700,000.

However, World War II was raging, and the demand for oil was acute. The federal government eyed the oil sands as an important asset in the war machine but wanted significantly increased production. The best way to do that was to move the plant to a richer, more malleable source of bitumen. Opposition pressure was mounting in Ottawa. "If one Adolph Hitler had control of the Athabasca tar sands, does anyone believe for a split second that he would be worrying about the cost of producing the gasoline?" asked Lethbridge MP John Blackmore.

Under war and economic pressures, the federal government took over Abasand in 1943. Ball had little choice, since he and his investment group could not cover the required upgrading costs. Ottawa paid no compensation to Abasand investors, but it did cover reorganization costs.

During Ball's management, Abasand had maintained a professional relationship with Clark's research council, exchanging useful information. Once the federal government took over, all interaction ceased. Even Ells, the federal man in the oil sands, found it difficult to learn what was happening at the project. In addition to ignoring the two best experts on the Athabasca sands, Abasand under the federal government had even greater woes. It became extremely difficult to attract and keep labour because the U.S. army paid better wages for the Canol project, a pipeline that was being built in the North and had a supply-shipping yard at Waterways. Soon Abasand was plagued with charges of mismanagement, which quickly became a political hot button.

Ball went back to the United States and took the post of special assistant to the Deputy Petroleum Administrator for War. He proved himself to be indispensable and went on to a stellar career, working on national U.S. energy laws. He also helped Turkey and Israel develop similar laws.

Ball's exit gave the province a reason to scold Ottawa. "Mr. Max Ball, an engineer who has been the promoter of this operation from the beginning, and who knew more about the physical operations of the process than anyone else, was immediately pushed out of the picture by the Dominion government and the plant put in charge of men who knew nothing about the process," said W. A. Fallow, Alberta's minister for public works.

It took another full year to get the machine working. Production at Abasand was more impressive than Bitumount, but not nearly enough to justify its expense.

In Ottawa, the federal minister of munitions and supply, C.D. Howe, said: "There seems to be some erroneous idea in the minds of many regarding these tar sands. Judging by what one hears at times, one would think that oil is running out of these sands, and that all that has to be done is to tap or pipe the oil and this country would overcome its serious oil shortage. The facts do not bear out any such idea."

In 1943, the federal government brought in General Engineering to redesign the plant, and the new company moved away from the McClave process. The news further fuelled suspicion in Alberta.

At the Alberta Legislature in March 1944, the provincial government demanded that Ottawa set up a Royal Commission to investigate activities at Abasand, alleging waste of public funds. Fallow went so far as to suggest systematic sabotage. In the eyes of the public, it was another example of the federal government failing to address the needs of Alberta. It was as much a political issue as it was a business or energy need. In Parliament, the munitions and supply minister was roasted, but C.D. Howe denied any direct involvement with the project, even though it had become a federal war effort. Now there was a call in Ottawa for investigation.

Then in 1945, a welder's spark burned down the entire plant, including the new 500-barrel-a-day separation unit. The total cost of rebuilding Abasand was estimated at $1.9 million, and the feds stalled. Ottawa decided in December that there was no point in competing with the provincial government, which was by then moving into renewed operations at Bitumount. In 1948, Ottawa sold off the Abasand assets.

Throughout this time, squabbling between the Alberta provincial government and Ottawa intensified over effective management and development of the oil sands. Part of the province's decision to get involved with Bitumount was that the feds had failed at Abasand. Successive administrations in Edmonton were all convinced of the importance of oil sands progress. Alberta took up Bitumount to prove to private investors that the oil sands offered a lucrative potential.

The Abasand plant was eventually swallowed up by Sun Oil, and in turn, that company's Alberta operations evolved into Suncor.

After Ball's death, Abasand was considered a mistake in an otherwise impressive career. Abasand was not referenced in his obituary.

Bitumania

The year 2002 marked the first year in which Alberta's oil sands output exceeded conventional crude production. Oil sands now produce about one-third of all oil in Canada. It is estimated that about 80 percent of the Athabasca oil sands can be explored and leased for production.

At 11°C, bitumen is solid like a hockey puck. About two tonnes of oil sands produce one barrel of oil.

Alberta is not the only region with oil sands. Melville Island in the Arctic has an estimated 500 million barrels.

CHAPTER TWELVE

Ernest Manning
Alberta's Longest-Serving Premier
Creates the Basis of Energy Policy

WHO OWNS THE GREAT RESOURCE THAT LIES UNDER ALBERTA, WHAT should be done with it, and how should any revenue be used? Those questions were among the most important that Premier Ernest C. Manning's government had to solve.

Manning entered politics and stayed in power throughout one of Alberta's most prosperous periods—and a good chunk of that prosperity came from oil and gas wealth. He was at the helm as Alberta graduated from a quiet homestead and farming economy to an energy contender. Yet as premier from 1943 to 1969, Manning also had to battle outside forces. U.S. industry wanted to exploit Alberta's riches, while the federal government wanted a national policy that ensured domestic supply.

The longest-serving premier in Alberta's history grew up on a Saskatchewan farm. When Manning got a radio in 1924, he heard a broadcast by Calgary preacher William Aberhart, whose fiery religious rhetoric won him the title "Bible Bill." Hooked, Manning moved to Calgary to join Aberhart's Prophetic Bible Institute. After graduation, he became Aberhart's right-hand man, sometimes filling in by running the institute, sometimes by handling the radio preaching.

When Aberhart became premier in 1935, 26-year-old Manning became the Social Credit Party's provincial secretary and the youngest cabinet minister in Canada. When Aberhart died in 1943, 34-year-old Manning took over as premier. Despite his youth, he gained a reputation for competence and integrity, his popularity bolstered by his own radio evangelism, including Canada's national *Back to the Bible Hour*, which had half a million weekly listeners. "Religion isn't something you keep on a shelf and only take down on a Sunday," Manning said.

He won the 1944 election partly by toning down the Aberhart hard line while sticking with conservatism. That in itself broadened his public appeal. In addition, Manning, like Ralph Klein later, impressed Albertans because he was so much like them—a working man. He bought a farm, and after the 1944 victory, Manning and a party official picked cabinet members while they shingled the barn roof, writing the names on lunch bags.

"I never got any satisfaction of making somebody mad if you could gain your end by congenial means," said Manning. "I've always thought there was great deal of truth in the old philosophy that says the greatest victory you could have over any enemy is to make him your friend."

On the energy front, Manning was tested early with the issue of what to do about the oil sands, specifically Bitumount and Abasand. Once it became clear that federal involvement with Abasand was a bust, the provincial government was forced to act. The huge northern resource presented an opportunity to convert Alberta's economic base from agriculture to big industry. Reluctant because basic Social Credit policy kept government out of business, Manning's government made a deal with Lloyd Champion's Oil Sands Ltd. to operate Bitumount as an experimental

plant. Before the experiment was over, Abasand was finished and Oil Sands Ltd. had bowed out of Bitumount.
The province was on its own.

Then in March 1948, with Manning coming up for
re-election, Atlantic No. 3 in the Leduc field blew out with
an initial 45-metre-high gusher, and it was a true maver-
ick. The crew desperately filled the hole with as much mud
as it could, to no avail. Over the next few days, smaller
gushers started erupting around the well site, and a pool of
oil began to form, creating an extreme fire hazard. Earth
and snow were piled into dikes to contain the growing
lake of oil. Public concern, and eventually industry worry,
grew with each week. Production in the area was curtailed. After the rig crew tried all it could to cap the blowout, Atlantic called in a U.S. expert, who not only failed to
cap the well, but made things worse.

Manning's government initially sat back and waited for
industry to solve its own problem. But now the rogue well
was threatening the future development of Alberta's biggest reservoir found so far, and the public was beginning to
worry about drinking water contamination. The Socreds,
heading into an August election, needed to resolve the
problem at Atlantic No. 3. The province's conservation
board, created under Aberhart, was under equal public
pressure to solve the blowout crisis. By early June, conservation board and oil industry authorities had the situation
better in hand and gave the nod for production to resume.
That gave Manning some breathing room to win his second
election. Then on September 6, the oil-softened surface
around Atlantic No. 3 gave way and the rig collapsed, snap-
ping electrical cables, firing sparks and setting off a massive
explosion and fire that shot flames 210 metres into the sky.
The story hit newspapers across North America and

Europe. The blaze was visible for 32 kilometres, according to witnesses. Huge injections of water eventually stemmed the flow of oil and gas. The fire and blowout were finally quelled on September 10, ending the biggest test so far for the province's conservation authority. After the crisis, the inevitable issue of liability emerged. In a series of negotiations aimed at avoiding unending lawsuits, the conservation board was able to negotiate a settlement that penalized Atlantic. With that out of the way, the government turned to its next burning issue, royalties.

Political flames had raged for some time over the province's introduction of bonus royalty bids—an attempt to bring in more revenue from energy. Under the program, lease bidders could offer a bonus royalty. Basic royalties were 15 percent, but in the rush after the initial Leduc find, bidders were willing to go higher to ensure they won. The first bonus contract went to New Yorker Renzo Falco, who bid $10,000 plus a 58.5 percent bonus above the regular royalty. Industry loudly opposed the bonus system, suggesting it would eliminate potential profits, and without earnings, investment would dry up—there would be no oil industry. The Socreds were forced to back down by an industry backlash. Alberta's royalty rate was set at 16.66 percent, or one-sixth of the total gross value of production.

Also at this time, one of the biggest questions facing Manning's government was whether gas should be sold elsewhere or kept at home for use by Albertans only. Manning created a commission to probe the issues and approved its recommendation that exports be banned until enough reserves were found to more than ensure Alberta's own needs. Yet before the 1940s were out, plans were on the books for hundreds of millions in export pipeline projects.

Some experts wanted gas kept in Alberta to fuel future industrial growth. Low-cost gas could be a lure to industry, they argued. Alberta Liberal leader J. Harper Prowse suggested: "Money realized from depletion of Alberta's natural resources should not be considered as racetrack winnings. It should be considered rather as a family inheritance to be handed on intact from one generation to the next." Prowse proposed government gas revenues be used to stoke a trust fund for Albertans, an idea picked up later by Progressive Conservative Premier Peter Lougheed.

For his part, Manning promised legislation to protect Albertans from high prices or depletion. After taking the province through the Depression, Manning maintained the view that energy was an opportunity to rebuild wealth in Alberta and wean the province off agriculture as the primary employer. The province was under pressure to rush Alberta resources into the U.S. Pacific Northwest before the Texans did and won all that potential revenue (a prediction that proved correct). Also at the time, Alberta couldn't produce enough investment capital to build a larger, value-added petrochemical industry, and eastern capitalists weren't interested.

Under 1949 legislation, Alberta had the right to approve export sales and also control flow. About the same time, the federal government brought in its own legislation, promoting the incorporation of pipeline companies, a move that Alberta viewed as a threat to resource control.

In 1951, the conservation board postponed hearings into export sales when it outlined that 133 billion cubic metres of gas reserves weren't enough the meet the province's requirement for Alberta self-sufficiency. As a result, exploration was stepped up to find the reserves to push the number over the requirement. Indeed, that supply was found.

Things changed again in 1951 when the federal government told Manning that Alberta gas was needed in Montana to fuel copper mining, an important commodity used in the war effort against communism, particularly in Korea. Manning put through legislation and a pipeline was in place that year. His energy policy gained public support. A Medicine Hat farm wife told *Time* magazine in 1951: "God knew that Mr. Manning would use the oil wisely, so He let it be discovered."

By 1962, Manning was in Los Angeles for the official opening of a 2250-kilometre-long pipeline that would carry Alberta gas. It was enabled at home by Alberta Gas Trunk Line (AGTL), which had been given a monopoly on gas collection in Alberta for export. AGTL was structured under legislation to maintain control in Albertans' hands. Manning devised the corporate plan himself in a bid to prevent federally incorporated pipelines from handling Alberta gas. In addition, TransCanada Pipeline Ltd. (TCPL) had completed a line into Central Canada and was lobbying for the right to export sales. AGTL gathered gas and handed it over to TCPL or Westcoast Pipelines at the border. Today, AGTL is part of Nova Corp., a company with thousands of employees and billions in revenues. Step by step, Alberta's gas lines were connected and eventually hooked up to export lines to the U.S. Controversy over export sales continues even today.

During the 1940s and 1950s, the Alberta energy boom increased provincial revenues and the personal incomes of its people. The province was now moving into a period of oil-fuelled wealth. By the 1950s, Manning's government had become an administrator of oil prosperity. Thus in 1957, the Socreds resurrected the Aberhart initiative for "Citizen Participation Dividends," a direct payment to each Albertan. For 1957, the payout from government coffers amounted to $11 million, some $20 for each person. Cheaters promptly went to several banks, presented identification, signed a form and took the cash, again and again. The province tracked down and convicted 323 people, including one who had collected 60 payments. The province tightened up the process in 1958, but it proved cumbersome, and Alberta's second round of oil prosperity payments was scrapped in 1959. Not until 2005 would a provincial government decide to try the scheme again.

When Manning quit in 1969, he handed over the premiership to the decent Harry Strom, but political change was already in the wind. A young Progressive Conservative had taken a seat among the Opposition and was about to make a bid for power. It was a sign of the times. While Manning continued his weekly *Back to the Bible* sermons on radio, Peter Lougheed was practising his television delivery. In 1971, Lougheed brought in a new Conservative government and set the stage for yet another round of battling with Ottawa over energy control. Manning had established a stable royalty program with a review every 10 years. It was typically Social Credit—set the rules and let industry go to it. Lougheed saw things differently.

After his political career was over, Manning created resentment among some Socreds by taking board positions with a number of companies, even a bank, anathema to the party that worked at a distance from such institutions.

Manning became the first Socred to be appointed to the Senate. His son Preston Manning later led the federal Reform Party.

At his retirement from politics, Manning addressed the accusations about his demeanour. "Over the years I have been portrayed by newsmen and commentators as an enigma—reserved, dour, cold and void of emotions. I am happy to report to you that none of these afflictions have ever caused me any pain."

Bitumania

By 1955, crude oil had replaced coal as Canada's largest energy source. Alberta first pipelined gas to Ontario and Québec in 1958. Today, Alberta supplies about 80 percent of Canada's natural gas and has huge storage capacity for natural gas and an extensive pipeline network. The Alberta Hub, a collection of storage and shipping points for natural gas, is considered one of the most important in North America, and the hub price is considered a benchmark.

CHAPTER THIRTEEN

Leduc No. 1
Imperial Oil Proves Alberta has Abundant Oil Reserves

IN A BIT OF BRAVADO, IMPERIAL OIL LTD. INVITED A NUMBER OF guests—dignitaries and reporters—to witness a predicted oil strike on a cold and blustery February day not long after World War II, about 16 kilometres west of Leduc. Word got around, and at the prescribed time two days later, some 500 people turned out at Mike Turta's farm.

The event didn't quite go to plan, but it did make history.

"The big business event of the 20th century in Alberta was the discovery of oil by Imperial Oil at Leduc on the 13th of February in 1947," Henry Klassen, professor emeritus with the University of Calgary's history department told the *Edmonton Sun*. "Imperial Oil Ltd., a subsidiary of Standard Oil of New Jersey and Canada's best-known and largest oil company, grew huge in Alberta as a result of this discovery. This event symbolized the major theme in the rise of big business in Alberta."

When Leduc No. 1 came in that day, it proved at last that there was a substantial oil reserve in the province.

It almost didn't happen. Rumours swirled that Imperial Oil, the major player, was about to quit its Western Canada play after 133 dry holes, costing $23 million, to instead concentrate solely on natural gas. Most of Canada still relied on coal for energy. The amount of oil that was consumed was mostly imported from the United States. Turner Valley's oil reserves were known to be depleting, and there hadn't been a significant discovery anywhere since 1936 in Turner Valley. Oilmen wondered if there was anything left to be found.

In Toronto, at the head offices of Imperial Oil, a tough debate broke out at a meeting of the company's technical committee. Some committee members argued for deeper wells. But others simply said the game was up—they weren't about to fruitlessly spend more corporate dollars on unlikely outcomes. But, in the end, they decided to recommend one last chance, a recommendation that was only approved after another bitter argument, this time among the board of directors. The stage was set.

The first hint of the resource in the Leduc region came in 1886 as geologist J.B. Tyrrell scouted the North Saskatchewan River. Along the way, he noted an area of "flattened beds." He reported to the director of the Geological Survey of Canada: "This report will, it is hoped, serve as sufficient guide to point out the extent, position and character of mineral wealth of the district." Yet Tyrrell, whose name is now on Alberta's famed dinosaur museum, didn't realize that he'd provided the first clue to the Leduc field because he was looking for coal seams. It wasn't until after the discovery of oil at Leduc No. 1 that oil company geologists spotted the same flattened beds first mentioned by Tyrrell.

Canada applied an Excess Profits Tax in 1917, and like any tax, it subdued investment. But World War II increased demand for oil. Drilling was encouraged in the war years, with the introduction of up to 50 percent in deductions against drilling costs on the Excess Profits Tax. The incentive spurred drilling in the prairies but produced little.

The problem in Alberta was that drilling had been too shallow, missing the productive Devonian structure deep below the surface. Deep wells, obviously, were more expensive gambles, and it was understandable the Imperial Oil board was reluctant to spend more after its numerous failures.

Following the board's decision, geologist Ted Link, among those who favoured deeper drilling, sent out a question- naire to 32 other staff geologists seeking their opinion on the best place to search for oil in the west. Most chose an area encompassing Calgary, Edmonton and Grande Prairie. Company landmen began taking up exploration rights in the region—but as quietly as possible in order not to flag competition. Imperial Oil had other reasons for being care- ful. Alberta landowners who owned property prior to the turn of century were entitled to a 12.5 percent royalty from any production on their land. Imperial Oil went about seeking surface rights, including a negotiated price per acre.

Imperial Oil gathered up rights to 80,936 hectares over a vast area, and then sent in the seismic crews. Two slight anomalies appeared, one near Pigeon Lake and another at a location near Leduc. Pigeon Lake seemed a more likely prospect, but Leduc had some other attractive factors. While the Pigeon Lake site would require the construction of an access road, Leduc was close to a highway. The latter was also closer to Edmonton and all the services that could be obtained there, and as well, it was closer to the North Saskatchewan River, a water source. It is interesting to note that the Pigeon Lake site was later drilled—and proved another dry hole. What would have happened had Imperial Oil gone there first?

But the Leduc site got the nod, and the toolpusher, or rig manager, Vern Hunter, was called in.

Records aren't certain about when Hunter got the nickname "Dryhole." In fact, his son has suggested that he made it up himself after Leduc No. 1. In any case, it stuck. He was known as Vern "Dryhole" Hunter because he'd been on so many failed drill sites. Hunter started out as a truck driver and clerk at Turner Valley, then got on the rigs as a roughneck, the lowest rank of labourer on a rig, and worked his way up to toolpusher.

Hunter was toolpushing for Royalite, the Imperial Oil subsidiary, in 1935, when the firm's regional manager, Walker Taylor, stopped by at 4:00 AM one night. Hunter was busy with a crew trying to fix a failed diesel engine. Walker asked Hunter why he just didn't let the crew do the work.

"It's pretty hard to sleep when you've got an engine broken down," replied Hunter. Taylor was so impressed that when he took a job on the huge Norman Wells field in the Northwest Territories, he took Hunter along as drilling superintendent.

Hunter followed the northern stint with a series of dry holes in Saskatchewan between 1943 and 1946. That last year, Hunter was ordered to pull his rig out of Saskatchewan, because Imperial Oil feared the new Co-operative Commonwealth Federation (CCF) government of Tommy Douglas would soon expropriate drilling equipment. Hunter's team moved to a location near Provost, where they spudded in for one last dry hole before being assigned to Leduc.

It was part of Hunter's process to meet a landowner before he began drilling. In an amicable meeting with

Mike Turta, Hunter offered to build an access road to the well site. But Turta wasn't willing to part with the cropland. Instead, the crew accessed the site through the farmyard. Turta was paid $250 a year, but two years later that was upped to $3000 a year to cover extra acreage.

(As a side note, Turta's 79-year-old father Anton became a millionaire in 1952 through a court ruling on mineral rights. Records and testimony proved that the term "petroleum" had not been included in rights reserved by the Canadian Pacific Railway when the land was first sold. The elder Turta bought the land in 1910, and though land titles clerks added the missing words later, the court ruled in Turta's favour. By that time, the Leduc field was covered with oil derricks. Anton Turta was awarded $5 million.)

Hunter was unimpressed with the geologists' choice of location. He suspected it was another dry hole because it was too close to Edmonton—his belief being that no well that close to comfort would produce oil.

In any case, his crew spudded in on November 20, 1946, determined to go down 2133 metres if they had to. Over the days, the engines roared, and the Turtas hospitably invited crewmen in for tea and treats, while in turn, the rig hands bought farm products from the couple.

At just below 1500 metres, the well struck some oil during a stem test. After so much failure, Hunter decided there was a chance for redemption, and so he went deeper, into depths that geologists of the day believed held no oil. In January 1947, Hunter's pessimism turned. "We knew we had a damn good well," he said. On February 3, a burst of mud and light crude shot into the sky and drenched a roughneck.

Expectations were now also high in management. Based on the information coming in from Leduc No. 1, Imperial Oil pressured Hunter to set a date for production. The company was hoping for valuable publicity. "I named February 13 and started praying," said Hunter. "It's always a mistake around rigs to say you are going to do anything at a particular given time—something always happens."

Out went the invitations: to the provincial minister of lands and mines, Edmonton mayor Harry Ainlay, Leduc mayor Leo St. Clair Gaetz, corporate big shots and media. On the morning of February 13, Hunter's crew began preparations for the 1:00 PM event, but as they were swabbing (sucking oil to the surface to begin production), they broke a shaft in the hoist. The crew had not in 133 holes ever had to swab before, and the hoist was accordingly old and unused. With no time for repairs, the crew began the long process of pulling out the swab and starting over. By 1:00 PM, a huge crowd had gathered, standing around in freezing temperatures. Imperial brought out coffee, sandwiches, pickles, cake and doughnuts to appease the impatient assembly. The set time passed. The crew continued its frantic work as 2:00 PM passed, then 3:00 PM. Ainlay gave up and went back to the city for a meeting. Mounties on scene bugged the rig hands: "When's it going to blow?" The big strike was beginning to look like another bust. But the crew knew they were almost there, bringing in Alberta's first major oil strike from a depth of 1544 metres.

"You could hear it like a train approaching when you put your ear to the pipe," Hunter later recounted.

Another crewmember recalled having a difficult time keeping people at a safe distance. Some had even brought bottles hoping to capture some souvenir oil.

At about 4:00 PM, as oil, gas, mud and chemicals streamed up, Hunter gave the nod to 22-year-old roughneck Johnny Funk, the youngest member of the crew. Funk swung a burning sack around his head and tossed it— *whoosh*, Leduc No. 1 burst into flames that shot 15 metres high and sent up a huge plume of black smoke, visible for miles and signalling a new age in Alberta.

The new well produced 41 barrels in its first hour and 40 in the next, suggesting it would produce 1000 barrels per day. Imperial Oil hosted a bash at the Hotel Macdonald in Edmonton, but Hunter was simply too tired to attend. He went home to bed.

Three months later, Leduc No. 2 hit oil at 1637 metres, confirming the Leduc field. But by then, there were already 10 other independent oil companies drilling in the area, and the huge American and British multinationals were moving in as well. Farmers, many of them European immigrants who had started with nothing and lived in poverty, reaped huge lease payments, beyond anything they could have imagined.

The rush was on. In June 1947, Imperial Oil announced a $50 million exploration program, mostly targeting Alberta. It also announced that it had bought a small refinery built in Whitehorse by the Americans during the war. It would be dismantled, shipped to Edmonton and reassembled. By the end of the year, there were 31 producing wells across the Leduc field, pumping out 372,427 barrels per day.

Hunter served as toolpusher on Leduc No. 3 before he was promoted to field superintendent in the region. He also went on to enjoy some minor celebrity, appearing twice on the CBC current affairs game show *Front Page*

Challenge. His picture appeared on an Edmonton transit pass, and a bar in Leduc was named for him.

Leduc was one of the richest oil deposits ever in Canada, a 200-million-barrel discovery, converting Alberta into a vibrant oil patch. Leduc No. 1 alone pumped out 317,000 barrels of oil and nine million cubic metres of natural gas and kept producing until 1974. Alberta's oil output surged from three million barrels in 1946 to 143 million barrels just a decade later.

Bitumania

The town of Devon, southwest of Edmonton, was born of the Leduc oil strike. Imperial Oil Ltd., looking to house an influx of workers, found that the town of Leduc, which had neither running water nor a sewage treatment facility, was unable to keep pace. Imperial bought a barley field from a farmer on the banks of the North Saskatchewan River to set up its own housing for workers, called Devon Estates (named after the Devonian formation, the depth at which oil was found). An early Devon rule prohibited residents from complaining about noise from the drilling. Devon is known as "Canada's Model Town," because it was the first to be approved by a regional planning commission.

CHAPTER FOURTEEN

Redwater and Pembina
The Leduc Discovery is Quickly Followed
by Two Bigger Finds

AFTER AN 11-YEAR DROUGHT BETWEEN ROYALTIES NO. 1 AND LEDUC No. 1, it was a relatively short period, about 19 months, before the next big discovery came in, this time at Redwater, northeast of Edmonton.

A quiet hamlet of 160 people in the summer of 1948, Redwater residents didn't know their little town was about to burst on to the national scene. Reports indicate that Imperial, Chevron and Shell all had earlier seismic evidence of the huge deposit, but discounted it. Historian Aubrey Kerr recalls the experiences of seismic crews searching the Redwater area. Many of the farmers in the area were poor immigrants who couldn't speak English and lived in huts with dirt floors. The crews had to talk to the farmers through their children, who had learned English at school.

Geologists of the time didn't understand that ancient Alberta, some 400 million years ago, was a vast, tropical inland sea, teeming with rich plant and marine life. Today, that seabed is buried and compressed into a tilted, saucer-shaped structure bearing fossil fuels. After Leduc No. 1, geologists and wildcatters had a better understanding of the Devonian reef, and a series of deep discoveries followed.

Imperial's scouts picked a spot on Hilton Cook's farm, a few kilometres northeast of Redwater. Kerr reports

Cook's biggest concern was that he wanted employment for his three sons, so Imperial hired them all. Toolpusher Fin Lineham, previously in Turner Valley and Leduc, turned up at the farm one day while son Jud was thresh-ing and pitching bales. "Fin Lineham came out to the field and took the fork away from me and offered me $1.20 an hour... I had no idea what the oil business was about," Kerr recounts Jud saying.

Imperial Oil spudded Redwater No. 1 on July 23, 1948, at least two years after the first seismic results had offered hints of the great wealth below. The oil firm's projected depth was 2134 metres, with an estimated budget of $180,000. The disappointed crew hit salt water at 871 metres and was starting to lose hope when nothing promising appeared through 945 metres. Then they moved into lime-stone and the drilling was quicker, showing spots of oil. Drilling was stopped for testing, and word started to travel inside Imperial Oil. When drilling resumed, more oil started to appear. On September 25, corporate officials brought 500 box lunches from Edmonton to meet with the crew and Redwater residents. Redwater No. 1 went into production on October 7 at 995 metres.

Initially, Redwater also produced a powerful natural gas smell. That didn't go over well in the region, especially because Atlantic No. 3 burning near Leduc could be seen from Redwater that summer. But after experiences in both Leduc and Turner Valley, where gas was thought to be a nuisance, knowledge was growing about the value and handling of natural gas. Redwater spurred the devel-opment of a series of pipelines to handle the valuable gas.

After Imperial Oil's Redwater production began, it didn't take long for the magnitude of the discovery to be understood. Eventually, the Redwater field would prove to be 32 kilometres long and five to six kilometres wide, with an estimated 1.3 billion barrels of oil in place—four times bigger than Leduc.

It was at this time that the Manning government resolved the dispute with industry over the bonus royalty program. The province introduced a sealed bid process with a cash bonus. In November 1948, the province auctioned Crown land rights at Redwater, earning $936,000 on 194 hectares. As the field proved itself, it became more valuable. The province sold another $7.8 million in rights in February and August of 1949. It seemed that all the Alberta oil players were there: Imperial, Royalite, British American, Dome, Atlantic and Texaco among them. At its peak, some 926 wells dotted the landscape.

The hamlet became Alberta's latest boomtown. The population soared to an estimated peak of 4000. It has levelled off to about 2000 today. The expansion brought new services, including a hotel, curling rink, beauty parlour and movie theatres. Redwater hosts an annual celebration called "Discovery Days" to honour its history. Many Imperial Oil staffers served Redwater in volunteer and official roles, such as sitting on town council. The company also donated land for recreational facilities.

What began in Leduc was confirmed in Redwater. Alberta was a major player in the world oil industry. By 1975, Redwater production had peaked at 180,000 barrels per day, but has since declined. Total output to the turn of the 21st century was about 800 million barrels, and though now slower and spewing a lot of water, Redwater is still producing. Through the mid-1950s, Redwater produced under its own pressure, but now the oil must be pumped and the water separated. In the late 1950s, the water problem resulted in the creation of the

Redwater Water Disposal Company, operated by Rice Engineering & Operating Ltd. The operation became one of the biggest water-separation companies in the world.

In the wake of Redwater No. 1, there was a rush to drill in the region. In 1949, a group of small independents found a 60-million-barrel deposit at Joseph Lake, southeast of Edmonton. Imperial Oil scored again at Golden Spike, southwest of Edmonton. Several other discoveries came in. Yet, the biggest of them all—Pembina—was still waiting to be found.

Arne Nielsen grew up on an Alberta farmstead and planned a life in farming. When World War II broke out, he was anxious to join up, but his father insisted that he finish high school. Nielsen then enlisted, but before he could be shipped to Europe, the war ended. He volunteered for the Pacific, but again, before he was posted, Japan surrendered and the war was over. However, Nielsen was able to use veteran's credits for his two years' military service to help pay for post-secondary training. He studied geology at the University of Alberta, and while at school, he got caught up in the excitement of Leduc and its promise of future discovery and potential wealth. In 1953, at age 27, Nielsen was district geologist in central Alberta for Socony-Vacuum Exploration Company, which later became Mobil Oil.

That year, Socony was offered a farmout deal by Seaboard Oil Company of Delaware to drill a deep wildcat in a rugged area in the Drayton Valley area about 26 kilometres from the nearest well. (Under a farmout deal, the owner of an oil lease contracts another company to explore and drill it for a share of what's found.) Seismic work at the Drayton Valley site had indicated an anomaly, but it was a big gamble. The cost of the well was estimated at $200,000. Nielsen was part of the group of geologists that prepared a report for Socony's New York head offices to recommend drilling. In that report, Nielsen suggested that the Cardium rock layer, previously disregarded, might contain oil. The Socony-Seaboard well was spudded in on February 23, 1953. At about 1615 metres, tests were ordered, and when the pipe was pulled, it was discovered that there was oil in the bottom 33 metres—the Cardium formation. However, it was only a slight indication, and the drilling crew was ordered to press on to the prescribed depth of 2865 metres. Nothing more of significance was found.

With no success at its total depth, the Socony-Seaboard well and the Pembina field could have easily been abandoned. But Nielsen and his fellow geologists advised taking a closer look at the Cardium formation, if for no other reason than confirmation and information. The plan was greeted with scepticism, but got the go-ahead.

The crew pulled back to the Cardium level for further exploration. Nielsen and other geologists on the job decided to try a new method that had been successfully applied in the U.S. called hydraulic fracturing, in which an oil and sand mixture is pumped under pressure into a formation. The process cracks the rock and allows any petroleum present to flow through the cracks into the well. The crew pumped in 1361 kilograms of diesel mixed with sand under high pressure. The attempt proved successful. On July 1, oil started to flow at a rate of about 72 barrels per day. However, heavy rains turned the region into a quagmire, and Socony-Seaboard was forced to shut down until September. When operations resumed, the well produced at 200 barrels a day.

A second Socony-Seaboard well was a dry hole, but the third also produced oil at the Cardium sandstone. Suddenly, an understanding of the new discovery began to develop. It was the first time oil had been found in Alberta in the Cardium formation, and it differed significantly from other oil reservoirs found so far. Leduc and Redwater were giant pools. Pembina was a thin wedge of sandstone in which a shallow layer of oil was trapped under any surface point. But the kicker was that it covered 2590 square kilometres, and that added up to the biggest oilfield found yet. The fact that the Pembina deposit is so thin adds to the legacy of the Socony-Seaboard well. It could have easily been passed through without notice.

As usual, word got out, and there was a rush by oil companies to buy land, start drilling and get in on the action. Under provincial regulation, much of Seaboard's reservation was cut into a checkerboard and sold to the highest bidder. Leases sold for as little as $500,000 and as much as $24 million. Over the coming years, a full half of all the wells drilled in Western Canada were in Pembina, and Drayton Valley became Alberta's newest boomtown. More than 70 oil companies set up operations in Drayton Valley, and in one year, the town's population soared from 75 to 2000 people.

Historian Earle Gray reports that $1 billion was spent developing Pembina, 5000 wells were drilled, geologists estimated the total reservoir at 8 billion barrels and the province may collect $1 billion in leases and bonuses before Pembina is done.

In Mobil Oil's own history, Nielsen recalls: "In those days, there was only one phone line that went into the Drayton Valley general store. We were concerned about our major competitor, Amoco, getting hold of our plans. Since my wife and I lived on the edge of Edmonton, the company set up two telephone poles in my backyard to receive the radio signals from the well site and ran the line into our bedroom where I deciphered the information. We also had cores under the bed. My wife was very under-standing, but the neighbours circulated a petition about the poles, and I had to go to each one to calm them down."

Nielsen received a series of promotions, and by 1967, at the age of 41, he was president of Mobil Oil Canada Ltd. He left Mobil in 1977 to head up Canadian Superior Oil. Eventually, they became the same company.

Bitumania

A typical Alberta rig crew includes, from junior to senior rank: two roughnecks, who work the drilling floor; a derrickman, or motor-man, responsible for machine operation; a driller, responsible for everything on or above the rig floor and drilling operations; and a toolpusher, who is the rig supervisor and boss.

In early 2006, the Canadian Association of Oilwell Drilling Contractors forecast 28,266 wells would be drilled in that year across the country, an all-time high. That was 17 percent more than the previous year. In 2002, another busy year, 14,459 wells were drilled. By late September 2006, the association counted 814 rigs. By comparison, there were 486 in 1997.

CHAPTER FIFTEEN

Eric Harvie
A Multi-Millionaire Alberta Oilman
Gives Away His Wealth

AT ONE TIME, ERIC HARVIE WAS BELIEVED TO BE CANADA'S WEALTHIEST man, but his real fame is in generosity. Harvie gave away most of his Alberta oil–gained wealth, including 200,000 cultural and ancient artifacts, to establish the Glenbow Museum in Calgary. By the same token, he staunchly avoided publicity and hated to have his name in the media. He lived modestly for his wealth, but also spent lavishly on his collections.

Harvie was born in 1892 in Orillia, Ontario, and studied law at Osgoode Hall in Toronto. While visiting his uncle, J.D. Lafferty, a former mayor of Calgary, he also articled in law under another uncle, James Short. The Calgary practice dealt with a range of oil ventures, and the youthful Harvie was caught up in the spirit of searching for oil wealth.

But World War I erupted, and by 1917, Harvie was in the trenches as a lieutenant with the 49th Battalion of the Canadian Expeditionary Force. At the Somme, during a battle at Courcallete, a shell blast buried him, injuring his elbow, knee and hip. Harvie was stuck in territory overrun by the enemy, and most of his fellow soldiers were dead or badly wounded. He crawled from hole to hole, hiding beneath corpses as enemy troops looted the dead. He stayed there until stretcher-bearers arrived. Harvie developed a condition known as "trench fever," which is caused by lice and produces symptoms similar to malaria. The fever recurred throughout the rest of his life. After a lengthy recuperation, he was seconded to the Royal Flying Corps, serving at training camps in Ontario and Texas before his discharge in 1919 at the rank of captain.

While he was serving in Ontario, he met Dorothy Jean Southam, from the wealthy Southam family, which owned a newspaper chain that included the *Calgary Herald*. They were married after the war, and Harvie set himself up in law practice in Calgary. His clients included Bill Herron's Okalta Oils, British American Oil Company, Dow Chemical, drilling contractors and a range of oil patch players. He bought in here and there and was a founding director of Okalta. By 1926, Harvie had so much personal investment in oil that he incorporated Managers Limited to handle his oil affairs and offer services to others. There were more failures than successes, but he slowly accumulated some wealth. It was nothing compared to what was to come.

Part of his practice dealt with the transfer of land under the Veterans Land Administration Act for soldiers returning home from war. The work gained Harvie a detailed understanding of laws pertaining to land and title. When he wasn't working long hours in his law practice, Harvie was an outdoorsman, hunting, fishing and trail riding. He also owned a ranch.

Throughout the 1920s and 1930s, Harvie invested in land, picking up properties in the Turner Valley oilfields, and began to assemble blocks of leases.

Then in 1943, he was offered a deal on property being liquidated by the British Dominion Land Settlement Corporation Limited, which in 1925 had taken over from a receiver title to 195,200 hectares of freehold mineral rights and 104,000 hectares of farmland, all in Alberta. British Dominion sold the farmland, but a 1931 venture formed to seek oil—Anglo-Western Oils Ltd.—didn't fare well, and by 1943 was in deep debt and tax woes. All of the properties were familiar to Harvie through his law practice. A representative of British Dominion, who had previous dealings with Harvie, was on his way to Winnipeg to make a deal on the lands, but met Harvie in Calgary at the last minute. It took Harvie 20 minutes to make a decision. His firm put up $23,739 to buy the properties and pay the transfer fees. Historian and writer Earle Gray said that it later proved to be the most successful gamble in the Canadian oil patch, and no one has ever owned as much oil and gas as Eric Harvie. By the time the deal was done, he was the fourth-largest freehold mineral rights holder in Alberta, after the Canadian Pacific Railroad, Hudson's Bay Company and the Calgary and Edmonton Corporation. At the time, Alberta's oil industry was well into the slump between Royalties No. 1 and Leduc No. 1. Chances of an oil strike anywhere seemed remote. Nevertheless, Harvie believed the vast properties would provide steady income from lease rentals, and there was always a chance that some other type of commodity might be discovered.

In 1944, Harvie set up Western Minerals, a holding company on his assets across central and north-central Alberta, and Western Leaseholds, to lease out subsurface rights. The Harvie family held 78.9 percent of Western Minerals. He sold minority stakes to office associates and other partners. In addition to its holdings, Western Minerals drilled the first wildcat in the Arctic Circle in 1957 and was the first oil company to find crude and natural gas in the Yukon in 1959.

In January 1947, Imperial Oil leased the Leduc No. 1 property neighbouring holdings from Harvie's companies. With a winner on its hands, Imperial Oil eventually took up leases on 77,200 hectares of Western Minerals rights for $2.23 million cash, option payments, a nine percent gross production royalty, plus a $1 per acre rental. That was just the beginning for Harvie's companies, because of course, it wasn't long before other explorers were taking out leases. And, on top of that, the Western Minerals holdings included land in the yet-to-be discovered Redwater giant. When that came in, Harvie hit the big time.

By the early 1950s, his personal wealth was estimated at $100 million, the equivalent of a billion or more today, and he could easily have been the richest man in Canada.

Now Harvie's attention turned to other interests in his life. "To neglect history is one of the shortcomings of civilization," Harvie once said. He had long been collecting Native specimens such as beadwork and arrowheads. This early collection was donated to the Luxton Museum in Banff.

Paintings, artifacts, medals, armour—anything with historical value—were all part of his collection and his vision of preserving cultural heritage. Harvie was known for voracious scouting. He scoured the world and never went anywhere without sending back crates full of new acquisitions—the last Model-T ever built, a set of Queen Victoria's bloomers, Sitting Bull's battle drum from the Battle of Little Bighorn, aboriginal robes, masks, drums. He continued his interest in indigenous people's pasts with artifacts collected from Central and South America, Australia and Africa. When he went to Egypt, a staffer joked, "I wonder where we'll put the pyramids." One staffer reported: "We were told to go out and collect like a bunch of drunken sailors." The stockpile started to fill up factory buildings around Calgary.

By 1955, Harvie had established the Glenbow Foundation, named after his ranch, to keep track of the collection. When Harvie needed assessment or archiving, he recruited the best people he could find. A friend joked that Harvie should leave his wallet at home when he travelled. Harvie replied: "I want to die broke."

Also that year, Harvie and his partners sold their remaining stake in Western Leaseholds for $18 million plus shares in Canadian Petrofina.

In an agreement negotiated with Premier Ernest Manning in 1966, Harvie donated the shares of the Glenbow Foundation (with its 200,000-item collection) to the people of Alberta with a $5-million endowment. Two years later, the Glenbow Museum opened in Calgary. In addition, Harvie contributed to a wide range of causes from zoos to cleanup campaigns for main streets in small towns. Harvie became a trustee and contributor to the Woods Foundation, named after former *Calgary Herald* publisher J.H. Woods. In addition to serving as legal counsel to the *Herald*, Harvie was also a director of Southam Inc., the newspaper's head company. The Woods Foundation was part of the initiative to establish the Banff School of Fine Arts and also contributed to the Calgary Zoo.

The University of Alberta awarded Eric Harvie an honorary degree in 1957, with the citation: "Mr. Harvie is one of those men who has been endowed with a sense of history, and he has the energy and ability to do something about it."

But all the wealth, collecting and charitable donations were giving him a public profile, as much as he wanted to avoid it. When Harvie complained to an Alberta cabinet minister about press reports estimating his fortune, the minister asked if the numbers were correct: "You know, I've never really thought about that," Harvie replied. Although he avoided publicity, reports suggest he cared little about image. Yet there is an account of Harvie complaining when he was charged $3 for a car wash instead of the $2.50 he had expected. When a couple left after working for 20 years as caretakers to Harvie, he deducted $5 from their final paycheque for the groceries they took with them.

In 1973, Western Minerals was sold to Brascan Limited for $32.5 million, ending a 30-year run.

Despite his wealth, Harvie lived in a humble bungalow in Calgary's Elbow Park and drove a banged up Studebaker. He died in 1975 at the age of 82. *Time* magazine described Eric Harvie as a rich man who "gave everything back and then some." The Crowfoot people named Harvie "Natos-Api," meaning "Old Sun."

Harvie made provisions for his family in a trust fund and gave what little was left of his estate to his charities. According to his biographer, Fred M. Diehl: "In effect, he died broke."

Before his death, he gave one interview to Peter C. Newman in which he offered a tidbit of advice: "Never throw away old socks, old underwear or old cars."

Bitumania

Canadian oil companies produced 136.4 million cubic metres of crude during 2005, down 2.3 percent from the previous year (the first decline in six years). Alberta production accounts for 66.5 percent of the national total, with one million barrels a day pumped out of the oil sands alone. Saskatchewan turned out 17.8 percent of total Canadian crude supply, while Newfoundland

and Labrador accounted for 13 percent from the Hibernia and White Rose offshore fields. Two-thirds of Canadian crude output is exported, and 99 percent of that goes to the United States. Canadian crude exports in 2005 amounted to $30.2 billion, compared to $25 billion in 2004.

CHAPTER SIXTEEN

Pipelines
Crossing the Border Creates More Conflict

ONCE YOU FIND OIL AND GAS, YOU HAVE TO MOVE IT. TODAY, members of the Canadian Energy Pipeline Association, which transport 95 percent of all crude oil and natural gas produced in Canada, move 2.47 million barrels of oil and 495 million cubic metres of natural gas daily. That product is worth a combined total of $202 million per day. Pipelines employ about 24,000 Canadians. The cost of pipelining energy compared to rail, truck or ship is minor. Oil and gas tend to be found in remote locations, away from the end user. Putting the two together has created an enormous infrastructure that snakes across the continent, and indeed, around the world.

Before pipelines, oil was gathered in cans, buckets, barrels…anything…and hauled by horse-drawn wagon, perhaps to a railhead. Once natural gas was discovered in Alberta, it wasn't long before pipelines were shipping it. Eugene Coste built the first pipeline in Alberta in 1912 to carry gas from Old Glory to Calgary and Lethbridge. By 1914, Turner Valley was in production, but because Coste had an exclusive contract for Calgary, that gas had no market. Once the automobile arrived on the scene, demand for petroleum products increased, and trucks started to handle some of the load. But then came World War I, and with it a huge spike in demand. Discussions began about wider distribution and small pipelines popped up here and there. But by 1949, when Leduc and Redwater had been confirmed as giant deposits, the issue of a cross-country line was at the top of the national agenda. And because such a line would cross provincial borders, it had to be under federal administration.

Among the top issues: which route would be followed, and should Canadian product be exported or saved for home use only? The shortest route from Alberta to Central Canada cuts through the northern U.S. states. But some politicians equated the basic purpose of pipelines to that of the railroad and wanted the entire route built within the country's own borders. It was about nationhood, they argued.

"Surely, it is in the national interest, regardless of cost, that the main pipeline carrying Canadian oil should be laid in Canadian soil," Progressive Conservative MP Howard Green of Vancouver said in the House of Commons.

In 1949, Imperial Oil applied to Ottawa for the incorporation of Interprovincial Pipe Line Company (IPL), and shortly afterwards, the federal government brought in the Pipe Lines Act. That was followed by approval for five pipeline companies, including IPL. Almost as soon as planning was underway for an Edmonton to Regina pipeline, major interest holder Imperial Oil, successful now at both Leduc and Redwater, began planning an extension to the port of Superior, Wisconsin, a $90-million project. Piping and shipping oil to Sarnia was estimated at $1 per barrel, saving $2.50 per barrel by rail. Once it was announced that the endpoint was a U.S. port and not on the Canadian side, a political storm erupted. Yet construction went ahead.

Canada's "Minister of Everything," C.D. Howe, was on hand October 4, 1950, near Edmonton when Premier

Ernest Manning turned the valve and sent Alberta oil down the pipeline toward the East. The new pipeline, Howe said, "...will stop a drain on our economy of at least $150 million U.S. dollars a year, which we are now spending for foreign crude." But it was already understood that more capacity was needed. The Superior terminal was scrapped, and work began to extend the pipeline all the way to Sarnia. By 1956, it reached Toronto, a distance of 3100 kilometres, the longest crude oil pipeline in the world.

In the 1960s, further expansions were laid to Chicago and other U.S. endpoints.

A series of major changes followed as IPL grew into a significant participant in North America's energy markets: in 1986, it took over Home Oil; in 1985, it completed an 870-kilometre line from Norman Wells, Northwest Territories, to Zama, Alberta (the first pipeline buried in permafrost); in 1994, it acquired the Consumers' Gas Company (still a major distributor of natural gas); and in 1998, IPL changed its name to Enbridge. Its shares are widely held. By 2005, Enbridge, active in Canada and the U.S., had more than 4400 employees and $8.4 billion in annual revenue.

The winter of 1956–57 changed the world scene on oil with the Suez Canal crisis, when British and French troops invaded the critical shipping zone over an ownership dispute. A blockade at the canal forced ships to take alternate routes, vastly increasing shipping distances for all products, particularly oil, thereby adding costs. Suddenly, Alberta oil looked good to Eastern Canadians who had relied on cheap imports. Once the crisis cleared and the canal reopened to traffic in 1957, Alberta felt a decrease in demand as foreign imports regained prominence. The debate over supplying Alberta crude to Montréal simmered on.

The Organization of Petroleum Exporting Countries (OPEC) supplied a twist to the story in the early 1970s. OPEC triggered a supply crisis that peaked in 1973, when the price of a barrel of oil imported into the refining hub at Montréal soared from $2.45 to $10.50. In September that year, Prime Minister Pierre Trudeau announced an extension of the IPL line from Sarnia to Montréal. Now, suddenly, the tables were turned, and Alberta oil suppliers weren't so keen. They had developed connections to closer markets in the U.S. Not only would they have to cut supply to good U.S. customers, but transporting to Montréal was more expensive. Nevertheless, the Montréal connection was completed in 1976 with federal financing.

In addition to eastern flow, Alberta's oil and gas also moved west over the mountains. Back in 1950, the U.S. was concerned that its Pacific Northwest lacked a pipeline supply connection. In 1951, the federal government gave approval to an application by Trans Mountain Pipeline, with initial shareholders Imperial Oil and Canadian Bechtel Ltd., to build a pipeline from Edmonton through the Yellowhead Pass via Kamloops to Vancouver and on to Seattle. The estimated price was $82 million. The proposed line crossed rugged terrain—mountains, rivers and thick forests. Construction became an engineering feat. When the pipeline opened in 1953, it helped fuel an economic expansion on the West Coast. Trans Mountain later changed its name to BC Gas and then Terasen.

In the early 1970s, a consortium of 28 companies, headed by TransCanada Pipe Lines and Alberta Gas Trunk Line, began preparation for a regulatory application on a pipeline from the Mackenzie Delta in the Arctic to the Alberta hub. The $10-billion project, officially unveiled as Canadian Arctic Gas Pipelines, would carry

135 million cubic metres a day. At the outset, northern groups, particularly the Dene, Cree and Inuit, complained. The aboriginals protested that mineral rights had been fraudulently taken from them, and they argued about environmental damage. Prime Minister Trudeau, facing an election, appointed former BC NDP leader Rodney Berger to head up a royal commission. The commission took two years, cost $4.5 million and heard 302 days of testimony from people across the North. In his treks across the North, Berger was sometimes forced to rely on canoe or dogsled. His 50,000-page report recommended a 10-year delay on any pipeline until land claims issues were settled.

More than 30 years later, in 2006, another round of hearings opened in the North, this time over a 1220-kilometre pipeline proposal, again from the North to southern markets. Connections through Alberta are included. The new endeavour is headed by Imperial Oil but includes ExxonMobil, ConocoPhilips, Shell Canada and the Aboriginal Pipeline Group, representing northern peoples with an opportunity for a one-third interest in the project.

In August 2005, Houston, Texas-based Kinder Morgan Inc. bid $6.9 billion to take over Terasen. The bid came as part of a series of U.S. corporate takeovers of Canadian energy companies, and critics were vocal in their opposition. In addition to picking up a stable and profitable gas distribution business, Kinder Morgan also believed that the acquisition would give it access to the Alberta oil sands, a resource of growing importance on the North American scene. Terasen shareholders and regulators gave approval to the deal, but not without some bickering.

"It is my belief that the sale of Terasen to Kinder Morgan is not in the best interests of Canadians or future generations," one shareholder said during the meeting to vote on the sale. "This is a utility we are selling, not a doughnut shop. We can choose not to eat doughnuts, but we can't make a choice about our utility." The takeover went ahead.

Inevitably, the issue of piping Alberta's natural gas directly to the U.S. was bound to surface. While several manufacturers established huge plants in Alberta based on cheap natural gas, there was still a significant amount of excess capacity. Debate on a proposed link to the U.S. naturally centred on increased costs to those suppliers should a giant buyer be added to the system. Some critics argued that part of the "Alberta Advantage" would be lost. In 1994, a group of like-minded people put together a proposal for the Alliance Pipeline, shipping natural gas from northeastern BC and Alberta to the U.S. Midwest. By the time the $5-billion project was ready for construction in 1996, 37 shippers had already been signed up. Construction began in May 1999, and the system was operating by 2001. Enbridge and Fort Chicago Energy Partners each own 50 percent. The 3687-kilometre pipeline carries 39.75 million cubic feet of rich natural gas to the Chicago hub every day.

Currently, Enbridge is developing a $4-billion pipeline to move oil sands crude from Strathcona County near Edmonton to Kitimat, BC, where it will be shipped to China and California—a further broadening of markets for Alberta's valuable resource. Accordingly, the 200,000-barrel a day project is called the Gateway Pipeline. Speaking to the Edmonton Chamber of Commerce in late 2005, Enbridge vice-president Jim Russell estimated the 1200-kilometre pipeline would pump out $160 million a year in economic benefit to Alberta and BC. Some $3 billion of the construction cost would be spent in the two provinces, he said.

The Gateway Pipeline is expected to create 5000 construction jobs and 75 full-time jobs on completion. It's due for start-up in 2009 or 2010.

Perhaps the biggest Alberta pipeline story of all was the one that didn't even happen in the province. In September 1999, seven Edmonton-area employees of United Pipeline Systems (and one American) were working on a line deep in the jungles of Ecuador when they were ambushed and taken hostage.

"They came out of the trees pretty fast, well armed," hostage Colin Fraser told reporters later. There were about 25 armed men and women in the assault group, hostages said. Their affiliation was never confirmed, but it's believed they may have been members of FARC, a Marxist guerrilla group that targeted North American companies active in the region.

What followed was a harrowing 100 days of captivity, during which the Albertans struggled for survival, battling dehydration and diarrhea. They were fed rotting meat from snakes and monkeys with perhaps some burned rice.

"We talked about our families every day," said hostage Neil Barber. "We stayed strong. We prayed. I think I'm going to church a couple more times."

They were moved often, sometimes forced to march for 30 hours on little sleep.

"We were guarded 24 hours a day," said Rod Dunbar. "Constantly knowing a machine gun is pointed at you, the fear is always there."

To help pass the time, the men first counted days and then began counting days until Christmas.

"Everybody stuck together," said Colin Fraser. "If a guy couldn't carry his pack anymore, at least three others volunteered."

While the hostages endured their ordeal, United Pipeline and the federal government worked feverishly for their release. Freedom came on December 19, after radio negotiations with the guerrillas. Reports suggested that United Pipeline paid a $3.5 million ransom, but the company refused to confirm the rumour. The hostages arrived home after a 14-hour flight to the Edmonton City Centre Airport, where a throng of well-wishers and media met them.

Bitumania

Three thousand years ago, ancient Chinese transported natural gas through bamboo pipelines to use for boiling sea water, part of a process to remove salt and produce potable water. Shafts of bamboo were cut in half down their length, and the inner core was stripped out. Then the halves were glued back together to produce an open pipe.

Today, natural gas moves through pipelines at about 40 kilometres per hour, compared to about five kilometres per hour for crude.

CHAPTER SEVENTEEN

Flamboyant Millionaires
Frank McMahon, Max Bell, Carl Nickle and Francis Winspear

ERIC HARVIE AND ROBERT BROWN WERE JUST THE FIRST OF A LONG LIST of oilmen who made a fortune in Alberta. Author Peter C. Newman called their breed "people who think big, live rich and live by the Darwinian rule that only the fittest and fastest thrive."

Frank McMahon

Before the 1950s were out, Frank McMahon had built an estimated fortune of $50 million and displayed it in his lifestyle. He spent between $75,000 to $100,000 on his daughter's wedding, including her gown, which alone cost as much as some homes in Calgary at the time. McMahon kept homes in Vancouver, Palm Beach and Manhattan. A racing enthusiast, the millionaire owned a Kentucky Derby winner and co-owned thoroughbreds with Bing Crosby. He also financed two Broadway hits.

McMahon grew up in the BC Interior but studied languages and business at Spokane's Gonzaga University, as Crosby's classmate. He dabbled in a number of failed businesses but never gave up. In 1938, he bought into some successful wells at Turner Valley, but for the most part, the new company produced dry holes. In 1947, McMahon got wind of a family dispute over a Leduc lease and hastily arranged a purchase.

It was at Leduc that McMahon's Atlantic Oils No. 3 rig blew out in March 1948, causing a public uproar. Atlantic No. 3 was out of control for six months before erupting into the biggest oil fire the province had ever seen. But McMahon wasn't about to be defeated by a rogue well. Once it was brought under control, he recovered as much spilled oil as possible, shipped it and still managed to make a huge profit. Now established in the oil business, Frank McMahon turned to his most ambitious project, a natural gas pipeline from the Peace River region to BC and the northwestern U.S. under a company called Westcoast Transmission. His brother, George McMahon, acted as Westcoast president. In the late 1950s, the McMahon brothers put up $300,000 of the $1 million needed for a new stadium for the Canadian Football League's Calgary Stampeders. The team's home field is today called McMahon Stadium. Frank McMahon lived into his 80s before succumbing to the effects of a lifetime of smoking and drinking. "Life was never guaranteed to be fair," Frank is quoted in his friend Ed Phillips' book *Guts & Guile*. "You have to grab it and shake it to survive. What is fair about living the way I have and end up having to bury two younger brothers?"

Max Bell

In his teens, Max Bell discovered an interest in racetrack handicapping, became an expert and learned to apply the same kind of risk-taking to business. His father owned four newspapers in Saskatchewan including the *Post* and the *Leader* in Regina and the *Star* and the *Phoenix* in Saskatoon. He sold those in 1926 to buy the *Albertan* in Calgary. Bell Sr. went on to further investments in newspapers, mining and oil, but suffered losses.

After university, Max Bell took a number of jobs in BC before returning to Calgary with enough money to buy a one percent gross royalty in Turner Valley Royalties. When his father died, Max Bell inherited the *Albertan*, which might have been a boon had it not been so severely in debt. But by then Bell was earning money on Turner Valley and was able to pay off the creditors and make the *Albertan* profitable. He continued to invest in oil, joining with friends to form Calvan Consolidated, which sold in 1955 to Canadian Petrofina for $40 million.

Throughout his life, Bell maintained an interest in thoroughbreds and co-owned a huge, successful breeding and training ranch near Okotoks with Frank McMahon. In 1959, he and a partner formed FP Publications, which owned daily newspapers across Canada including the *Globe and Mail*.

Max Bell was obsessive about fitness and exercised throughout his life, sticking to plain foods. He never smoked nor drank and was generous to his Presbyterian church. In 1972, Bell died at age 60 of brain disease. He established the Max Bell Foundation, which makes significant grants to health and education institutes.

Carl Nickle

Carl Nickle, the founder of *Nickle's Daily Oil Bulletin*, once gave a helicopter to one of his grandchildren.

Before his career in journalism, Carl Nickle worked in a shoe store, then in a Depression relief camp. While reporting for CFCN Radio in Calgary, Nickle earned a reprimand for picking up the story of the scandalous love affair between the Duke of Windsor (later King Edward II) and American divorcée Wallace Simpson. He was transferred to the oil beat just as the Turner Valley story was unfolding.

The Turner Valley success energized him to create the *Bulletin*, providing all the industry details. With an investment of $62, Nickle started the *Bulletin* as a one-page typewritten sheet. It struggled for years, with Nickle earning as little as $90 a month. But after Leduc No. 1, *Nickle's Daily Oil Bulletin* became important reading and listed oil companies, banks and government staff among its subscribers. Maintaining his interest in oil ventures, Nickle eventually began his own investing. Historian Peter C. Newman suggests that Nickle garnered $130 million worth of oil and gas wells.

A history posted on the bulletin's website suggests that it was the first to report the Canol Project, the top secret U.S. army pipeline to fuel the navy at Alaskan ports, in 1943. That report provided the first hint of the project to President Franklin D. Roosevelt. The project was supposed to be secret to prevent Japanese interference, so Nickle earned another reprimand, this time from the FBI via the RCMP.

Nickle was elected to Parliament for Calgary West in 1951 for the first of two terms, partly on a platform of keeping government out of the oil business.

Francis Winspear

A concert hall in downtown Edmonton carries the name of Francis Winspear. His fortune was estimated at about $100 million, and like other Alberta tycoons, he gave much of it away. Winspear supported the University of Alberta, hospitals, sports and arts. He had wide business interests, with ownership or control in about 40 companies, including Gold Standard Oils, which was a shareholder in Great Canadian Oil Sands. Unhappy with both the Liberal and Progressive Conservative parties, political-minded Winspear began discussions with colleagues that led to the founding of the federal Reform Party (led by Preston Manning, and including in its MP ranks future Conservative Prime Minister Stephen Harper). Winspear underwrote the 1987 Western Assembly in Vancouver, which created the Reform Party.

Bitumania

Indian Oil and Gas Canada is a federal "special operating agency" responsible for managing energy rights on aboriginal lands. In the 2005–06 fiscal year, the agency collected $271.5 million in royalties, bonuses and rent on behalf of aboriginal groups. It took in $1.5 billion in the seven years leading up to 2006. Some Native bands have started their own oil and gas firms to reap further rewards. At the end of 2005–06, the agency had 17 aboriginal-owned energy companies holding rights to 163,000 hectares of land under 167 subsurface agreements.

CHAPTER EIGHTEEN

Suncor
The First Major League Player in the Oil Sands

RICK GEORGE IS ONE OF THE OIL SANDS' BIGGEST STARS. WHEN HE took over as president and CEO of Suncor Inc. in 1991, at the relatively young age of 41, he brought a completely different style and attitude to the company compared to the typical conservative Alberta oil leadership. He talked to employees. He respected environmentalists. He looked for new solutions. It may have been just what the Alberta oil sands needed. George was certainly what Suncor needed.

"I was quite a young CEO, so in 1991, I would have been 41 years old. I felt I was going to have to live with all my mistakes. I knew that," said George.

There had been fires, worker fatalities and embarrassing leaks into the Athabasca River. The massive conveyer-belt operation was producing oil at a cost of about $19 per barrel when the world price was about $15 per barrel. George had hardly settled in before there was a $16-million fire at Suncor's upgrader. Then a midwinter electrical failure sent $10-million worth of equipment into deep freeze. "I try to forget it," grumbles George. He had tough work ahead to fix Suncor, an oil sands pioneer.

The history of the oil sands began with not one, but two big problems: technology and politics. By the early 1950s, no large operating plants had been established. In 1953, while scientists and politicians were trying to get things moving, Abasand Oils, Canadian Oils Ltd., Champion's Oil Sands Ltd. and Sun Oil Co. of Philadelphia formed a consortium called Great Canadian Oil Sands (GCOS), which would be Suncor's predecessor. Sun Oil was a big integrated company and was considered an innovator and a risk-taker. "Integrated" means it had everything along the oil spectrum from exploration to production to refining to selling. It already had operations in Eastern Canada, including the Sunoco gas stations. GCOS spent $1.4 million on research before its first plant was built between 1964 and 1967 for $220 million. Suncor's own historical record describes the investment as a "daring venture into an unknown field" and as the largest single private investment in Canada to that time.

"This is a great challenge to the imagination, skill and technological know-how of our scientists and engineers," said J. Howard Pew, a U.S. oil magnate and Sun Oil president and chairman. "I am convinced this venture will succeed, and that it will be the means of opening up reserves that will meet the needs of the North American continent for generations to come."

The GCOS plant opened on September 30, 1967, with Alberta Premier Ernest Manning on hand, boasting of the importance of the event. It was the world's first commercial-scale oil sands mining and upgrading facility. But in its first five years, it lost $90 million, battling fires, freeze-ups and breakdowns along the way. It took 12 years to turn a profit. Indeed, the oil sands do not easily give up the prize.

Suncor officially formed in 1979 when Sun's entire Canadian operations amalgamated with GCOS. Then, in 1981, Sun sold 25 percent of its interest in Suncor to the

Ontario provincial government. (Ontario divested its interest in 1992.)

Rick George was born in Brush, Colorado, northeast of Denver. He played football, married his high-school sweetheart, got a civil engineering degree and worked a few jobs in the U.S. before Sun Oil picked him up to develop an offshore oil platform in the North Sea. In 1991, after a decade honing his skills in the UK, George was hired by Suncor.

"The CEO before me was Tom Thomson," George said. "Tom had cancer and knew about it. He recruited me out of London to come in and replace him." Thomson's energy quickly faded, and he died shortly after George came in, a sad memory: "Tom was a real mentor to me."

It was a time of low morale and questionable prospects for the oil sands.

"Suncor, in the Sun Company portfolio, was an under-performing asset," said George. "It had, on average, a five-percent return on capital for the better part of a decade, prior to 1991. The mission I got was kind of very simple. They said, Rick, this has got a five-percent return on capital, and of course, the cost of capital is eight percent to 10 percent, so you've got to find a solution. That's as fundamental as it got."

George brought with him an optimism that had been missing at Suncor, partly by establishing a corporate vision and a five-year environmental plan. He also established a policy of recruiting the best minds in the Canadian oil patch, including some people that could have done his job. "It just makes more sense than having one brain at the top telling 3000 people what to do," George told *Canadian Business* in 2002.

"When I first came here, a lot of people in the oil sands thought we would shut down. It was like a process where necessity is the mother of invention. I said, listen guys, if we don't find alternatives to this, we're going to have to shut this operation down. Suncor would have become a very small company."

One of the biggest changes was switching from the drag-line system to truck and shovel. The new system used giant shovel machines that could be moved to remote places to dig for oil sands, while the biggest dump trucks in the world hauled the stuff back in. As a result, the extraction plant was able to efficiently serve a range of up to 50 kilometres, compared to about two kilometres previously. The change trimmed costs down to about $16 per barrel but also cost 400 jobs. Distraught, George delivered the bad news himself to staff in Fort McMurray.

"We did a detailed study on what our alternatives were and what technology was available," recalled George. "One of the things that came out of that was this move to truck and shovel. It doesn't sound like a huge advance, but it was the start of the whole thing.

"First of all, it was tough getting $120 million out of the board to make the technology switch, because at a five-percent return, they weren't really up for putting that kind of money into this thing. *That* was the first challenge." The appropriation was approved in 1992, and the new system was in place two years later. "The second one was getting it implemented. And then the third was the resulting lay-off of 400 people. It was a very painful process. The net result of all that was we reduced our cash operating cost by about $5 per barrel and return on capital improved, so then we could attract new capital. We became progressively more competitive, vis-à-vis against the conventional oil producers."

George and the Suncor management team developed an even longer-term plan, looking as far as 50 years ahead. Part of the plan was gearing Suncor for expansion.

"We really developed a vision," said George. "Listen, this company, these assets, are going to be here for 50 or 100 years. If you think about that, then you take a different approach. We started talking about values, beliefs. We set very clear long-term goals, not based on short-term commodity fluctuation prices. We talked to the NGOs [non-governmental organizations] and tried to find a middle ground.

"Right after truck and shovel, we started talking about doubling our cash flow and earnings every five years, our shareholder value, every five years. When we first came out with that, people thought it was a stretched target. It turned out that it wasn't a stretch. In fact, since we became a public company in 1992, we've been up on average 30 percent a year every year since."

Patti Lewis, a Suncor communications officer, recalled the change in corporate culture: "Before, you had a short-term focus, because we were on survival. You were just like, what do we need to do to keep in business? To try to squeeze out the oil and maintain your cost. When we brought in those trucks and shovels and brought our costs down, we were able to lift our heads up and look beyond our plant gate. We looked at different issues of our business, the different communities and stakeholders that we impacted."

The company went public in 1992, when the government of Ontario sold its shares in a public offering, and

Sun Co. reduced its Suncor holdings as well. The following year, Sun began selling off its remaining stake.

Environmental groups were surprised, and they raised red flags. George responded to their complaints. The result was a compromise on emissions that enabled Suncor to get its planned expansion project moving ahead of schedule.

Suncor applied to regulators in 1994 for the massive Project Millennium. Expansion got underway that year with a huge acquisition of leases to add eight billion barrels in reserves.

George also moved the head office from Toronto to Calgary in 1995.

"It was obvious to me that you can't effectively run an oil company from Toronto, in the sense that the majority of our assets were here," he said. "This is where the heart of the oil patch in Canada is." It also helped that the Ontario government had sold its shares, so the move wasn't subject to provincial politics.

Controversy rained all over the Millennium program as its costs ballooned more than a billion dollars beyond original estimates. Yet, Millennium increased production capacity to 225,000 barrels a day.

"We made the decision to go with project Millennium in 1998, right when crude was around $12 a barrel," said George. "There were a lot of doubters. Other companies were trying to pull back where they could. We made a very gutsy call, being counter-cyclical at that point. By the time we brought it on in 2002, oil prices had gone up and it was successful. We got beaten up by you [the media] and your colleagues, our shareholders and our board and everybody else, because the initial cost estimate was $2.2 billion and the project came in at $3.4 billion."

But George believes Millennium will go down as one of the cheapest expansions in oil sands history.

"If you look what people are now paying for 100,000 barrels a day of upgrading capacity, the numbers are three times as much."

Lessons learned, Suncor now has a major projects group, with about 400 staff, that concentrates solely on managing the capital plan. Suncor's 2006 capital spending was estimated at $3.5 billion.

Suncor still operates on what staff call "Rick's Mantra": increase production, reduce costs and reduce the environmental footprint. Indicative of its commitment, in 2000, Suncor unveiled a $100-million investment in alternative and renewable energy sources during the coming five years. It opened wind farms in Magrath, Alberta, and Saskatchewan within that period.

The company, which began as GCOS in 1967, produced its one billionth barrel in 2006, with average daily oil sands production at 260,000 barrels a day. By 2008, Suncor plans a 350,000-barrel-per-day output. It has applied to regulators for a third upgrader, a key component in increasing production to 500,000 barrels a day by 2012. In 2004, Suncor officially opened Firebag, an in-situ steam-assisted gravity drainage (SAGD) facility about 40 kilometres northeast of the original plant. SAGD is a process developed by an Imperial Oil scientist to reap oil from deeper deposits.

Suncor employs more than 5000 people spread over four business divisions in Canada and the United States:

oil sands, natural gas production in Western Canada, downstream refining, marketing and retail in Ontario and the same in Colorado.

Bitumania

It may seem a paradox, but in order to produce energy, Alberta's oil sands producers need significant amounts of...well, energy. Trucks and machines, plants and steam generators, the camps for workers—they all need power, heat, light and hot water. Today, the primary feedstock is natural gas, but with dwindling supplies, there is a constant debate on alternative sources. One of those alternatives is nuclear power. And it's gaining some credibility in Alberta, with politicians and oilmen alike. Even Premier Ralph Klein has suggested that a nuclear plant in the Athabasca region may be the solution to the oncoming supply squeeze. Among the benefits of nuclear power are that it is emissions-clean as opposed to pollution-causing gas or coal-fired energy plants and has a long-term cost advantage. One problem, beyond the usual concerns surrounding nuclear energy, is a requirement for large amounts of water, already a concern in the Athabasca region with oil sands demand. In any case, Atomic Energy of Canada Ltd. is on record saying that it's done the homework on building a nuclear plant at Athabasca.

CHAPTER NINETEEN

Dome Petroleum Ltd.
Crushing Debt Puts an End to
a Canadian Success Story

"SMILING" JACK GALLAGHER SPENT THREE DECADES BUILDING DOME Petroleum into a giant in the Canadian energy industry, only to see it collapse around him in a few years. Even when forced to sign off on a bailout package that effectively ended his career at the company he founded, Gallagher impressed observers with his grace and charm as he thanked them. The Dome crisis reached to the highest level of government, threatened Canada's major banks, influenced northern energy development and stung small investors.

Charismatic and relentless, Gallagher relied on skills he'd honed travelling the world for Shell and Standard Oil of New Jersey (now Exxon) when he became the first and sole employee of Dome Exploration (Western) Ltd. The company became Dome Petroleum Ltd. in 1958. At its peak, Dome employed 3000 staff and had billions of dollars in assets.

Gallagher grew up in Winnipeg and studied engineering at the University of Manitoba before switching to geology, sensing there was more opportunity in that discipline, partly because Prime Minister R.B. Bennett's government launched an initiative to explore and develop northern mineral resources.

In 1936, Gallagher took a summer job with the Geological Survey of Canada scouting the northern wilderness. The thick forests and vast terrain made an impression on the young man that never left him.

"The great thrill was that you were opening up country white men hadn't seen before," said Gallagher. "It was a tremendous experience for a young man to get in there and see the vastness of Canada and how little it had really been explored."

After graduation, he accepted a survey tour as expedition leader, receiving a raise from $2.50 per day to $2.85. For the most part, he worked with only one or two other people, living on little food and giving names to the lakes and rivers they discovered.

He joined Shell in California in 1937. For a decade, he travelled the world as an oil company geologist, but remained determined to return to Canada to open the North to oil development. Transferred to Egypt in 1939, Gallagher's work for Shell included a period in which he was on loan to the British Eighth Army—at one point finding a deep deposit of desperately needed fresh water. He joined Standard Oil for two years in Egypt and Palestine before moving on to tour the Peruvian Andes. There, he was able to convince unfriendly aboriginals to act as guides through the Amazon headwaters. He even found caches of Japanese arms while hunting the Ecuador jungle.

Gallagher was high in the Andes when his driver fainted from altitude sickness and their truck crashed into a rock wall. The accident broke three of Gallagher's vertebrae, and no medical help was immediately available. Eventually, the broken spine fused on its own, but he remained in pain the rest of his life. Gallagher was known for his double-clasp handshake, which he used to counter those men who grip and shake too hard. And his secretary made it one of her duties to help him put on or take off his coat. Despite the chronic pain, Gallagher remained athletic, even in his senior years, running, jogging, skiing and golfing.

In 1944, Gallagher was rebuffed in his attempt to gain some access rights in Ecuador. In an early example of his ability to play politics, Gallagher sought out the external affairs minister, gained a meeting with dictator Jorge Ubico and won letters that granted the permission he needed as well as some much-needed mules and canoes.

Gallagher admitted later it was likely that the Standard effort in the region was just as much about finding oil for itself as it was to supply the U.S. navy should the Panama Canal be taken out in conflict. Gallagher was under no delusions that Standard would use his work to help out the CIA's predecessor, the Office of Strategic Services (OSS), led by General Bill Donovan.

"Unofficially, I guess we were really working for Donovan's OSS," he said.

Standard then sent Gallagher to Harvard for further study, and he went on to do a short stint at Imperial Oil beginning in 1948, but he felt adrift.

It was in 1950, when Gallagher was 33, that a group of investors approached him and offered an opportunity to manage their affairs as the first employee in the newly formed Dome Exploration, a subsidiary of gold producer Dome Mines Ltd. of Ontario (which had significant U.S. ownership). With gold prices depressed at the time, the Dome owners decided it would be prudent to invest in other businesses. They were encouraged by the Leduc find in Alberta. Among the hundreds of oil companies that sprang up after the Leduc strike, Dome was one of few to survive.

Dome Exploration was headquartered in Toronto, but Gallagher set up a Calgary office. He slept on planes and dashed about from corporate meetings to oilfields. He chose drill sites himself, and Dome's first two wildcat wells, at Drumheller and Provost, were modestly successful. Gallagher began to build a respected team. One of the earliest people hired was 19-year-old Maurice Strong, who went on to wealth and an international career that included heading up the newly formed Petro-Canada, a stint at the United Nations and chairing the 1992 Rio de Janeiro conference on the environment.

Gallagher became a fixture at the Calgary Petroleum Club, where a lunch special consisting of a turkey salad sandwich, tinned fruit and cottage cheese was named after him.

Although profitable, most of Dome's discoveries were small—the company was constantly looking for a big strike and never found it. (Despite all of Dome's northern effort, it was Gulf that made the first discovery of significant Arctic deposits and that only after the Dome collapse.)

In the middle of 1951, Dome issued its first initial public offering (IPO). Dome issued 500,000 shares at $11.22 each in Canada and $10 each in the U.S., followed by a second offering in 1955. It never paid a dividend, plowing cash flow back into operations. Gallagher bought his first shares in the 1951 offering and continued to invest over the years, even when stock was low. By November 1981, he and his family owned 5,292,220 shares worth $134.3 million—which dropped to $15.9 million by the end of 1982.

Throughout the 1970s, Dome grew primarily by take-over, and its listed share price rose accordingly. Dome Petroleum shares worth $380 in 1954 had grown to $120,000 by 1981.

Gallagher now applied the political talents he had honed while touring the world for Standard Oil by developing key relationships with government ministers. Methodically, Gallagher drew up lists of important ministers and government staff, then set about meeting them and gathering information. He spent a lot of time in Ottawa, and as his contacts in government grew, so did his reputation. Eventually, Gallagher was asked to sit on the Canada Development Corporation board of directors, thus enabling him to gain government contacts that became important later when he began dogging Ottawa for concessions to explore the Beaufort Sea. Whereas the general consensus was that there was nothing of significance to be found in the North or that it was too expensive, Gallagher maintained his belief that huge oil and gas reserves lay in the Arctic.

In 1974, Gallagher received a letter from Minister of Northern Affairs Jean Chrétien promoting Dome initiatives in the North. The federal government was also anxious for northern development, for political reasons but also to increase revenues. Chrétien's letter suggested that if Dome completed the required environmental studies (a time-consuming and expensive endeavour), permission would be granted for exploratory wells. Based on that, Dome spent $130 million for two drill ships and support vessels.

Also based on the government's need for a northern presence, Gallagher began pressing his government contacts to lobby for tax incentives. The result was the Frontier Exploration Allowance, introduced in the Donald McDonald budget of March 1977, which became known as "super-deletion" or the "Gallagher Amendment." The allowance applied to wells costing more than $5 million and diverted government revenues for three years.

Meanwhile, in Alberta, Dome had established a gigantic gas system, hooking up pipelines and setting up straddle plants to remove liquids that producers could not extract profitably. Part of that strategy included buying up a 49 percent stake in TransCanada Pipelines Ltd. and rebuilding the company. When Bill Richards came in as Dome president (Gallagher remained as chairman) in the late 1970s, Dome went on its biggest expansion spree. As the company's fame spread, so did Gallagher's profile. He was dubbed "Smiling Jack" because he often showed his impressive grin.

In September 1961, Dome became the first company to drill in the Canadian Arctic when it spudded in on Melville Island. Initially, Dome made money by using its expensive ships to drill for other companies under contract, which proved a profitable venture, and by leveraging land concessions as part of the deal. Throughout its history, Dome applied a successful strategy of leveraging other companies' investments to its own advantage.

Trouble finally hit in the early 1980s under the combined impact of the National Energy Program and Dome's acquisition of the Hudson Bay Oil and Gas Company, known as "H-Bog," with good cash flow and massive holdings adjacent to Dome's own. H-Bog was a descendant of the venerable "Company of Gentlemen Adventurers," and the Hudson's Bay Company still had a stake. But H-Bog was paying 60 percent of its earnings in taxes, while Dome had $1.5 billion in tax credits stemming from oil and gas search incentives. Thus, Dome could seize H-Bog and protect some of that rich cash flow from taxation.

The first problem: the H-Bog takeover project was set in motion just before October 28, 1980, the day federal Finance Minister Allan MacEachen delivered the budget that included the NEP. Richards called the NEP "confiscation without compensation." After Dome's shares got nailed and Richards took heat, he admitted: "The government didn't receive it too well. I think one learns from these things that what you say may be correct, but it doesn't always pay to say it." Because Dome was only 35 percent Canadian owned, the terms of the NEP meant that its exploration credits were zapped.

Dome had four drill ships on the Tuktoyaktuk Peninsula waiting to head out for the 1981 winter season. But without federal incentives, and instead a $240 million bill, it couldn't afford to move.

H-Bog was 52.9 percent owned by Conoco of the U.S., while HBC had 10.2 percent, and minority shareholders held the rest. Dome tried to convince Conoco to accept a friendly offer in which Dome would buy up Conoco stock at a premium. Then, as a shareholder, Dome would trade Conoco's own shares to Conoco. Thus Conoco could retire the shares (hopefully boosting the value of the remaining stock) and take a tax credit. Dome would take Conoco's H-Bog stock in trade. Unimpressed, Conoco executives were angry when Dome bid for Conoco shares on May 5, 1981, offering 65 cents for shares that were then trading at 50 cents.

Conoco called in lawyers and financial advisers, and the result was a drawn-out affair. "That delayed the takeover and created all the animosity that developed during the period; I think if we had recognized that problem, we probably never would have moved on it," said Gallagher. Conoco chairman Ralph Bailey complained to shareholders that action should be taken to ensure U.S. citizens were not victimized by Canada depressing the value of its assets. He argued the Dome plan was simply a tactic to acquire H-Bog at a bargain. But the Dome offer brought in a 21 percent Conoco share, forcing Bailey into talks. In late May, a group of Dome officials flew into Conoco's Stamford, Connecticut, headquarters where the two sides played a bit of a spy game. Dome's team was concerned that all its talks were bugged and left the offices when they needed to place a phone call to Gallagher. They also posted a guard on the corporate jet to ensure it wasn't bugged as well. Tense negotiations set the price on H-Bog; the total cost of the deal was more than $2.3 billion. Gallagher personally phoned each chairman of Canada's four biggest banks (Royal, Toronto-Dominion, Canadian Imperial Bank of Commerce and Bank of Montreal) looking to round up the money. The four banks went ahead with a loan on Dome's pledge of H-Bog stock to back it. (But Dome already had $2.65 billion in long-term debt. When interest rates began rising, as high as 23 percent in the summer of 1981, the drain caused by its debt ran the company dry.)

Desperate to gain control of the final 47 percent of H-Bog, Gallagher met with famed Canadian billionaire and English baron Ken Thomson, who was also the controlling stakeholder in HBC, but Thomson spurned the offer. More tense negotiations led to a deal on November 3, 1981, with minority shareholders.

Just as things were set to go, MacEachen's second budget came down November 12, closing a tax loophole vital to the H-Bog deal. The Dome team had to scramble around Ottawa to allow its H-Bog takeover to proceed with a pass from MacEachen.

Dome immediately set about trying to reduce its debt. To appease its bankers, Dome tried to sell $1.5 billion worth of U.S. assets, but because of falling world prices, offers didn't even come close to meeting the asking price. Soon, the Canadian banks were getting jittery, particularly when Dome came looking for more. The company was forced to turn to a syndicate of U.S. banks to finance the purchase of the last 10 percent of H-Bog. The U.S. banks demanded H-Bog shares as collateral, a difficult move because the same shares were already pledged to the Canadian lenders. Realizing they had been caught in a pinch, the Canadian banks consented to the U.S. bankers' terms, but renegotiated their own loan terms, including shortening payment periods.

Scotiabank, which had initially avoided exposure to Dome, then got dragged into the story because it had an existing loan to H-Bog prior to the takeover. Scotiabank played hardball and exercised its right to $40 million in repayment, leaving the other four banks further aggrieved. Dome had no further assets, so the big four were forced to dole out the $40 million to Scotiabank.

The H-Bog takeover became official in March 1982, and before the ink was dry, Dome was back asking for $80 million to help pay its bills. Aghast, the banks refused.

By the end of March 1982, Energy Minister Marc Lalonde was talking to the banks about the company's difficulties. A Dome failure would not only be disastrous for the Canadian economy, but would cripple the federal government's energy endeavours in the North.

Soon, Dome was desperately working just to survive. Among its attempts to raise cash was a bid by subsidiary Dome Canada to sell the northern fleet, a move that further troubled the banks.

By May, the banks and the federal government were in meetings to discuss a Dome bailout. In June 1982, Dome's total debt reached just over $7 billion. The situation worsened in July, when a BC provincial New Democrat rose in the legislature to suggest the Dome situation might cause one of the big banks to falter. Over the next few days, all the banks felt a run as the public tried to pull money out. Eventually, the Dome situation began to affect the Canadian dollar, causing it to fall on foreign markets. Struggling in the wake of the H-Bog buyout, Dome cut salaries and wages, laid off staff, sold assets and delayed bill payments

In September, the Dome board held a tense dinner meeting with its bankers in which bailout terms were explained to a horrified Gallagher. The deal required Dome to issue debentures convertible into common shares at $2 each, at a time when Dome shares were trading at $5.25. The next day, at a board meeting, Dome's directors suggested that staff members (Gallagher and Richards) be excluded from further negotiations. Negotiations dragged along for about a week, during which the Bank of Montreal made it clear it was poised to put Dome into receivership.

"It's pretty difficult to negotiate with a gun at your head," Gallagher said.

Dome's board managed to squeeze out slightly improved terms, but the game was up. When the deal was announced in September 1982, shareholders basically got nothing and were predictably outraged, setting up a committee to fight the deal.

The Dome story had become a crisis. On September 29, 1982, at CIBC in Toronto, Gallagher signed away control of Dome, which he had built up over 30 years. Now he was vilified, because he'd lost $118 million in a year. On April 8, 1983, Gallagher relinquished his role at Dome.

Part of the final bailout package was a one-year remission of taxes, resulting in an estimated $1 billion loss in expected government revenues. The concession was later bitterly criticized by Auditor General Kenneth Dye: "There is something very wrong with a system that allows a $1 billion policy decision to be made by way of a tax expenditure with Parliament having so little information on the transaction. We are, after all, talking about public money provided by Canadian taxpayers who elect MPs to look after their interests."

In the end, Dome's new management team, sent in to salvage the company, was eventually forced to sell. Buyer Amoco Corp. of Chicago got Dome for $5.5 billion, giving secured creditors 95 cents on the dollar, unsecured creditors 45 cents and common shareholders $1.47 per share. British Petroleum later swallowed Amoco.

Gallagher died at the age of 82 in 1998 in Calgary's Rosedale Hospice after a drawn-out bout with cancer. The dazzling smile that lighted Canada's biggest energy company was finally dimmed.

Bitumania

In the 2005–06 provincial budget year, energy royalties, bonuses and land lease sales provided a record high $14.4 billion in revenues to the Alberta government, on total revenues of $34.6 billion. Of the total, oil sands provided $1.2 billion in royalties. The province built the budget on the assumption that world oil prices would average US$60 per barrel. They skyrocketed well above US$70 per barrel.

Energy products accounted for 70 percent of Alberta's $66 billion in exports that year.

CHAPTER TWENTY

Peter Lougheed
A New Premier Fights for Alberta's Rights

THE ENERGY CRISIS OF 1973–74 CHANGED THE WORLD ORDER AND had a major impact on Alberta's future oil development. To fully understand the battle that emerged between Premier Peter Lougheed and Ottawa, it is necessary to set the world scene.

At the outset of the 1970s, the price of crude oil had not really changed since the 1920s. From about 1860 until 1950, the United States dominated production, with almost half of world output. Also, the U.S. had important allies in world oil politics, giant multinational corporations known as the "Seven Sisters": Exxon, Mobil, Standard Oil of California, Gulf, Texaco, Shell and British Petroleum. Spread across the globe, they sought and produced oil and kept prices reasonable at home. Subsidiaries of the Seven Sisters imported oil into Canada.

In 1960, Saudi Arabia, Iran, Iraq, Kuwait and Venezuela created the Organization of Petroleum Exporting Countries (OPEC) to bring up prices and wrest control of oil. After all, the vast majority of the stuff was from their land. Who were these Americans and British to tell them what to do with their natural resources? OPEC set out to negotiate higher world pricing. Initially, the major oil companies managed to play off one OPEC member against another, thereby ruining any endeavour that required full participation for success. If most members of the cartel decided to withhold supply in order to drive up prices, the effort was defeated if even one other member used it as an opportunity to pick up extra sales. Only through complete solidarity was OPEC action effective.

Canada's oil scene was tied to world events. Although Turner Valley and Leduc established an industry in Alberta, producers had a difficult time exporting beyond the West. Initially, Alberta production levels weren't anywhere near enough to keep pace with national demand. Prior to the 1947 strike at Leduc, Alberta provided only 10 percent of national consumption, while most of Canada's oil was imported from the U.S. or Venezuela. A decade later, Canada was processing 654,000 barrels of oil per day, with about 347,000 of that from domestic supply. The rest was imported, almost entirely from Venezuela.

Pipelines from Alberta were built to British Columbia and Ontario. However, those tubes carried Alberta product into direct competition with U.S. supply in the Pacific Northwest and with cheaper imports from Venezuela in Eastern Canada. It was to be an ongoing, nagging problem.

Conservative Prime Minister John Diefenbaker appointed Toronto businessman Henry Borden in 1957 to report on Canada's energy industry, including the issue of critical importance to Alberta: how much of the nation's market should be reserved for domestic producers? The biggest part of business for Canada's big oil companies, subsidiaries of American multinationals, was in refining and marketing. Most refining was done in the Montréal region, fed by cheap foreign oil imported through parent companies stateside. Alberta producers, trying to expand sales and establish a stable market, wanted a bigger piece of Eastern Canada. They lobbied Ottawa, hoping for an

import tariff on foreign oil plus some pipeline enhance-
ments. But the eastern consumer won out; the Borden
Inquiry did not recommend a tariff. Borden did, however,
suggest a barrier along the Ottawa Valley, beyond which
foreign oil could not cross, giving Alberta producers unin-
hibited access to all markets west of the line. Diefenbaker's
government introduced the Borden recommendation as
policy in 1960, the same year that OPEC formed. In his
1979 book, *The Blue-Eyed Sheiks*, author Peter Foster
points out that as a result, Ontario consumers paid more
for oil than their Québec neighbours, in effect a subsidy
to Alberta producers—a point that Wild Rose oilmen
were happy to ignore.

The United States under President Richard Nixon in 1970
applied import tariffs on Canadian oil. Quickly, though,
the tariff was removed because by 1972, American demand
outstripped its own domestic supply, and the U.S. needed
oil. U.S. production peaked in 1972, yet its appetite for oil
grew unabated. Thus America became an oil importer.

Canadian oil exports to the U.S. leapt 22 percent compared to the year before, up to one million barrels a day.
Now Canadian opposition grew. U.S. parent firms controlled most of Canada's oil industry. The majority of
Canada's oil production was flowing out of the country,
right at the height of a worldwide "energy crisis." Anti-
American sentiment flared.

In October 1973, Egypt and Syria entered the Sinai and
Golan Heights, taken by Israel in a previous conflict six
years earlier. Israel battled back until the United Nations
was able to enforce a peace later in the month. Angry Arab
countries began talks about using oil economics as a weapon
of war. Among their initiatives was a Saudi announcement of a 10 percent cutback in output and a total embargo

on supply to the U.S. and the Netherlands. But, in a move that showed continued weakness in OPEC member solidarity, the Iranian Shah took the opportunity to increase his nation's sales to bolster government revenue.

World oil spot prices were about US$3 per barrel in 1973, but by the start of the next year, the price had almost quadrupled, standing at an OPEC-imposed price of US$11.65 per barrel. Oil had changed world politics.

In 1973, federal Energy, Mines and Resources Minister Donald Macdonald in the Pierre Trudeau Liberal government applied a federal oil export tax, based on a National Energy Board report suggesting that Canadian production could not meet both domestic and foreign demand in coming years. New premier Peter Lougheed expressed the Alberta government's outrage, calling the move a flagrant breach of faith.

"This appears to be the most discriminatory action taken by a federal government against a particular province in the entire history of Confederation," Lougheed told the Canadian Club in Calgary. "Why just an export tax on oil? Why not on lumber from British Columbia, potash from Saskatchewan, nickel from Manitoba, pulp and paper, asbestos and gold from Ontario and Québec?"

Washington was equally angered when it learned that the smaller amount of Canadian oil crossing the border would be sold at world prices. Congress moved to censure Canada, so Macdonald was dispatched to Washington to appease the Americans. Macdonald pointed out to his U.S. counterparts that Canada was paying world prices for its imports for the East, so it could hardly charge a lower price for its exports. The energy minister also warned the Americans that Canada would be phasing out exports altogether, and any future oil sands development would be for domestic consumption only. At the height of the crisis in 1974, oil prices had quadrupled. The price of gasoline skyrocketed. Motorists lined up at gas stations across the U.S. and tempers flared. There was rationing; some stations ran out of gas. Oil-rich nations, particularly in the Middle East, began nationalizing their energy industries. Inflation soared in the U.S. People would never think about energy the same way again.

The stakes had been raised.

Peter Lougheed was elected premier of Alberta in 1971, unseating the Social Credit Party, which had held power for 36 years under Bill Aberhart and Ernest Manning. Lougheed was from an upper-class Calgary family, grandson of James A. Lougheed, a Turner Valley investor and federal politician. His maternal great-grandmother was Métis. A branch of the family (that spelled their name differently) established the Lockheed aircraft corporation in California. His grandfather, Sir James Lougheed, had convinced the CPR to take him on as the company's Calgary lawyer, and he bought prime properties in the then tiny hamlet before the railway's arrival. Two princes, later King Edward VIII and George VI, stayed in the Lougheed Calgary mansion. Peter was 10 years old when the family mansion was lost in foreclosure. That event would be a factor in his future battle for Albertans' rights.

Lougheed studied law at the University of Alberta in Edmonton, then ran back punts for the Canadian Football League's Edmonton Eskimos before heading off to Harvard for an MBA. He did a stint with Gulf Oil in Tulsa, Oklahoma, where he saw what an oil bust does to an energy economy. Back in Alberta, Lougheed worked for Mannix Corporation, a huge, privately owned Calgary firm with interests in construction, pipelines and oil, before heading into legal practice.

Alberta's Conservative Party was floundering when Lougheed jumped into politics in 1965, taking the Tory leadership in 1967. At the outset, Lougheed planned radical change. He intended to increase the province's take on energy exploitation in order to fund development in health, education, research and other areas of industry. Part of the scheme was to diversify Alberta's economy away from a reliance on oil. (Diversification has been an issue with almost every Alberta government.) He wanted a stable, industrialized economy, built on its oil-based heritage. And just as importantly, Lougheed wanted Alberta business to thrive on its own, without the overpowering Toronto Bay Street influence. He set about building respect for Alberta. And he would do that, he said, by taking control of "our own resources."

On August 30, 1971, 43-year-old Lougheed set his home barometer to "change" and then went off to vote. Youthful in comparison to the long-standing Socreds, the new Conservatives mastered the use of television and media, applied splashy campaigning techniques. They used their inspiring image to lead the party to an election victory of 49 seats to the Socreds' 25.

Among his first promises, Lougheed pledged a complete overhaul of provincial royalty rates in order to increase annual revenues by $90 million. However, royalties were included in oil and gas lease contracts, most of which were in force until as far off as 1980. Lougheed took the rare approach of holding public hearings before the full legislature in 1972 and then scrapped the Socred royalty.

"In our view, the Social Credit government made a very serious error in judgement in 1948 when it agreed unnecessarily to insert into petroleum and natural gas leases a specific provision that the maximum royalty rate payable by the producers would be limited to 16-and-two-thirds percent or one-sixth of gross production," Lougheed said. The new government policy made no restrictions on maximum royalties on future leases, offering some relief to those holding existing leases.

Next, Lougheed challenged the pricing system for natural gas. The premier argued that natural gas being exported out of Alberta was underpriced by perhaps as much as 40 percent. He called for Alberta input on national energy policy and for observer status at energy trade negotiations with the U.S.: "If Alberta poker chips are involved at the poker table, we will be at that table." The federal government dismissed Lougheed's demands, noting that provincial jurisdiction on natural resources ended at its borders.

After an enquiry into fair pricing for natural gas, the Alberta Tories released a 1972 position paper resulting in increased royalties (to 21 percent) on new wells. Existing leaseholders had to pay a reserves tax but could opt for the higher royalty instead. Wildcat wells were free of royalty for five years. The increases infuriated oil companies and soured relations with the new premier.

Throughout the energy crisis, Ontario Conservative Premier Bill Davis traded barbs with Lougheed. He had taken issue with Alberta's move to increase prices through higher royalties and demanded talks with the provincial government. Lougheed held off, forcing Davis to travel to Alberta, a move seen by some commentators as symbolic of the whole conflict.

"The East is used to us Westerners coming to them on bended knees," Lougheed said. "Now we are holding the high cards in terms of energy, and we plan to use them."

Davis threatened to go to court. He complained to the Energy Resources Conservation Board. And he threatened a continued political backlash. Lougheed held his ground; he even threatened to cut off supply to the East.

In August 1973, Imperial Oil announced a substantial increase of 40 cents per barrel. The total increase in nine months was 95 cents, or 32 percent. Public reaction was a ruckus. Thus in September, Prime Minister Pierre Trudeau floated the framework for a new national energy policy. The plan included erasing the Ottawa Valley line and building a new pipeline to bring western oil into Montréal. Ottawa now clearly realized that if world prices continued to skyrocket, it would be better off maintaining some control over domestic supply. In addition, the federal government applied a five-month freeze on gas and energy products and slapped a 40 cent per barrel tax on oil exports. But Alberta oilmen were now no longer so keen to see their oil moved into Montréal, when better prices were available from export sales to the U.S.

When Donald Macdonald, the energy minister, announced that Canada's now limited exports would fetch world prices, he also told Alberta that the increase would be kept in federal coffers as an export levy. Indignant, Lougheed refused to back down from confrontation.

"Jobs, both existing and future, are in jeopardy in Alberta today. We have to try to protect the Alberta public interest—not from the Canadian public interest—but from

Central and Eastern Canadian dominance in the West," Lougheed said.

The political oil battle with Alberta, simmering for years through events at Turner Valley and in the Athabasca oil sands, now moved into dramatic action. The tension was heightened by the world energy crisis, which had worsened with the October conflict in the Middle East.

In December, Trudeau's government officially introduced the new energy policy, delivering another tough blow to Alberta oil producers and the provincial government. Trudeau made no bones that he was challenging Alberta.

In 1974, the infamous "Let the Eastern Bastards Freeze in the Dark" bumper sticker popped up in Alberta, further inflaming the cross-country rhetoric. For Albertans, the slogan was an embittered war cry. For consumers in the East, it was a symbol of Alberta greed. The words were actually an adaptation of "Let Those Yankee Bastards Freeze in the Dark," seen on bumpers in Louisiana and Texas as those states debated the distribution of natural gas to other states. Alberta geologist and independent oilman John Frey saw the tag line and thought a revamp could provide comment on Alberta's similar debate. He printed a few hundred copies and handed them out to friend at the Calgary Petroleum Club. "It struck me as a reasonably lighthearted expression of a serious concern," Frey said later. The public uproar shocked him. "I felt like I'd peeled back an ordinary bandage and unexpectedly discovered a deep, gangrenous infection underneath."

In March, a First Minister's meeting resulted in an increase of $2.40 on the domestic oil price to $6.50 per barrel. The province then fired back by announcing a 65 percent royalty on oil, tripling existing rates. Oil companies were by this time reporting huge increases in profits because of higher world prices. The public viewed the whole thing with scepticism and corporate mistrust.

Then in May 1974, the federal government took another shot in Finance Minister John Turner's budget. Alberta's 65 percent take on oil would simply be ignored for federal taxation. Deductibility of the provincial royalty was cancelled, and federal rates would apply to the entire oil price, regardless that Alberta had already taken 65 percent. It was a bombshell. The Liberal government fell without New Democratic Party support for the budget, but was re-elected. Turner reintroduced the budget, with royalty non-deductibility, in November, but by then it was too late. The Canadian oil industry had been devastated. Exploration slowed to a trickle.

Both governments eased their demands in the coming months, though Alberta continued to assert its right to set prices. Alberta planned to give back some royalty money because of the federal non-deductibility and also brought in tax credits and exploration incentives. The two levels of government were even forced to work together to save the proposed Syncrude oil sands project when major partner Atlantic Richfield pulled out. Alberta and Ottawa together invested $600 million to get the project moving.

Lougheed was re-elected by a landslide in 1975, confirming his popularity and public approval for his tough stance against the federal government. He won two more elections in 1979 and 1982. He quit as premier in November 1985 and resigned his Calgary West seat the following February. But before he left office, there was to be yet another significant clash with Ottawa. This one was over the National Energy Program.

Bitumania

After Premier Peter Lougheed increased Alberta's take on its energy resources, the province's revenues ballooned. As a result, the Lougheed government established in its 1975 budget the Heritage Savings Trust Fund. The fund was set up with an annual $1.5-billion endowment and had three divisions, one for commercial investments, another for promoting diversified businesses in Alberta and the last for capital projects such as hospitals and parks. By 1979, the fund had a base of $4.7 billion and was growing at a rate of $1.5 billion per year. It gave loans to other provinces at rates they may not have otherwise been able to obtain. In March 31, 2006, the fund was worth $14.8 billion. The fund's investment income now supports the province's priority spending programs.

CHAPTER TWENTY-ONE

Imperial Oil
Canada's Energy Giant

THROUGHOUT THE HISTORY OF ALBERTA ENERGY, ONE NAME POPS UP over and over again: Imperial Oil Ltd. The giant in Canada's oil patch, Imperial Oil began as a small Ontario private firm, bought into Turner Valley, found oil at Leduc and Redwater, invested in the Athabasca oil sands and finally, with more than 100 years behind it, moved its head office from Toronto to where the real action is, Calgary.

In February 2006, Imperial Oil, citing higher revenues for gas and bitumen particularly from its Cold Lake heavy-oil operations, reported a 2005 net income of $2.6 billion, a record high for the company. The previous high was $2.052 billion in 2004. Revenue for 2005 was $27.797 billion, compared to $22.408 billion the year before.

That's a long way from the $25,000 that the company began with in 1880.

Canada's oil industry began in Enniskillen Township of what is now Ontario in the 1850s, where "gum beds," well known for centuries to local Natives, were analyzed and discovered to be bituminous deposits. As development began, Canada's first energy boomtown emerged, called Oil Springs. Soon, a larger field developed at nearby Petrolia.

Frederick Fitzgerald, an area businessman in control of the London Oil Refining Company, and a group of 18 colleagues merged 12 refineries and some oil wells to start Imperial Oil on April 30, 1880. It was a bid to better withstand wobbling market prices and competition and to fend off takeover by billionaire John D. Rockefeller's Standard Oil. They each put in $25,000 cash. The company was chartered to "find, produce, refine and distribute petroleum and its products throughout Canada." Fitzgerald was named Imperial Oil's first president.

The new company dismantled 10 refineries in favour of two, in Petrolia and London (the latter burned down and was abandoned). Imperial Oil subsidiary Royal Oil Company sold kerosene for coal lamps under the brand name Royalite, which later became the name of another Imperial Oil subsidiary in Alberta. As the company went about its business, Standard Oil was persistently bidding for takeover, a basic Rockefeller strategy: get rid of competition by buying them. Standard bullied Canada's railways into giving it preferential rates and bought up oil companies and refineries around Ontario, shutting most of them down. Imperial Oil was slowly falling prey to Standard Oil's relentless campaign. It didn't have the financial depth to meet the Standard Oil onslaught.

With no other buyers available, Fitzgerald went to New York and secured a deal under which Standard Oil acquired 75 percent of Imperial Oil. For its part, Imperial got all of Standard's Canadian assets, but its master was American. When Standard Oil shut down the Petrolia refinery, this left its Sarnia plant as the only refinery in Canada. By 1917, under President Walter Teagle, Imperial Oil had become an integrated oil company operating across Canada. It opened its first service station in 1907, in Vancouver.

In its early history, Imperial Oil was a reluctant explorer— it was much more content to let other wildcatters do the work and then move in. When Archie Dingman and Bill Herron struck gas at Turner Valley in 1914, Imperial Oil owned 90 percent of the nation's refineries and controlled 75 percent of all petroleum sales. Teagle eyed the speculation in Turner Valley with typical Imperial Oil interest: "If there is any likelihood of paying production being developed in Canada, we should, if possible, try and arrange to be in on the ground floor with leases of our own, so that from the very outset, we might occupy as important a position as producers of oil in Canada as we now occupy as refiners and distributors." However, an Imperial Oil geologist investigated and sent back a less-than-glowing forecast. Imperial turned its interest elsewhere. It concentrated on freehold properties because of federal restriction against granting leases to foreign-held (other than British) companies.

The year 1920 proved to be a big one for Imperial. An exploration team led by Ted Link, who became a leading geologist in the search that resulted in the Leduc strike, hit a gusher at Norman Wells in the Northwest Territories. And, at Turner Valley, Herron and Dingman's Calgary Petroleum Products (CPP), hurt by a fire and in financial trouble, was looking for rescue. Imperial set up the Royalite Oil Company, holding 75 percent of its shares while CPP had the remainder, and acquired CPP's assets.

By 1923, Imperial Oil had grown into Alberta's largest oil company. That year, it opened a refinery in Calgary with a capacity of 4000 barrels per day.

Royalite rebuilt the burned out Turner Valley plant, got operations going again and, by 1924, was supplying gas to Calgary. The subsidiary went on to further success at Turner Valley with its 1924 discovery of oil, sparking the second boom in that region.

Soon the automobile was everywhere, and Imperial Oil moved along with the trend. By 1931, it had 299 service stations operating across Alberta.

Unfortunately, Imperial Oil went through a period of sustained exploration failure—133 straight dry holes. The company drilled its first wildcat well in 1917, which was followed by failure after failure through to 1947. In that period, the company spent $23 million in the West, accounting for a quarter of all drilling and half the geological work in the region, yet all it had was shares of the depleting Turner Valley field and the Norman Wells field, which was too far from markets to profitably deliver the product. Imperial was ready to abandon the West when a desperate meeting of company geologists, including Link, recommended one last attempt at Leduc.

The February 13, 1947, discovery at Leduc No. 1 enabled Imperial Oil to become a corporate big shot in Canada, particularly in Alberta. Leduc was followed with success at Redwater, and soon Imperial Oil was moving into pipelines: Interprovincial and Trans Mountain at the outset. Imperial Oil also established a major presence in Calgary with its regional offices. It opened a glitzy headquarters in Toronto in 1957.

Despite those successes, exploration costs still outweighed revenues. Imperial Oil sold its International Petroleum subsidiary in 1948 to raise $80 million, and the following year sold Royalite for $15 million as well as some other Turner Valley assets. Also in 1949, it sold oil and gas leases at the Viking-Kinsella field. That was all followed with a 1951 share offering that raised another $80 million. Processing and refining still offered the highest revenues for Imperial, much more so than exploration and recovery.

Accordingly, the company established an Edmonton refinery in 1948 with the most advanced technology available. By 1950, Imperial Oil's Alberta crude production was 13 million barrels, 48 percent of the province's total. One year after the Redwater success, Imperial's Alberta refineries were producing 21,000 barrels a day, and that increased to 28,000 barrels a day by 1954.

Testing began in 1964 on Canada's first in-situ recovery by Imperial Oil staff at its Cold Lake operations. The Cold Lake deposit on Alberta's eastern border north of Lloydminster is estimated at 44 billion barrels of oil in place, but it's heavy and it's deep. Imperial's test injected steam into a deep well to loosen the oil and pump it to the surface in what became known as the "huff 'n puff" method. In 1979, Imperial Oil applied to regulators for a $7-billion, 135,000-barrel-a-day mine and upgrader project. Cold Lake operations were stalled by political wrangling between Alberta and Ottawa over energy policy, but a reduced version of the project was up and running by 1985. Today, Cold Lake is the world's largest in-situ oil operation in the world, with 3800 wells connected by 600 kilometres of pipelines and an average daily production of about 130,000 barrels. Imperial at Cold Lake produces about five percent of Canada's annual crude supply.

In 1972, contruction began in Edmonton on a new refinery to replace four others, the existing facility in that city plus others in Calgary, Regina and Winnipeg. Completed in 1976, the Strathcona refinery in east Edmonton can process up to 195,000 barrels of crude per day. In 2003, Imperial undertook a $650-million upgrade at its four Canadian refineries to reduce sulphur in gasoline in order to meet federal initiatives. That was followed in 2005 and 2006, with a further $500-million upgrade at the refineries to meet standards for reduced sulphur in diesel fuel.

When the world energy crisis erupted in the early 1970s, oil companies became public enemy number one, and a Canadian oil company with an American parent was particularly vile. Imperial Oil was suddenly on the defensive. The company went on a public affairs campaign to brighten its image. In 1976, it advertised: "Like to guess how much profit Imperial Oil earns on each gallon of petroleum products it makes and markets? If you guess one or two cents a gallon, you're close. Actually, in 1975, the figure was less than one cent a gallon."

Imperial Oil continued to develop its Canadian assets. In addition to conventional and heavy oil operations, Imperial is involved in the Athabasca oil sands, is the lead in the proposed Mackenzie Delta pipeline and operates 2000 Esso service stations across the country.

In late 2005, Imperial Oil announced that its Toronto head office would be shifted to Calgary, affecting 500 of its 1500 staff in the Ontario capital. The move was interpreted in Calgary as another indication of the city's status as the mecca of Canadian oil. It was also expected to spur a short gallop in Calgary's real estate, already one of the hottest markets in the nation.

Imperial has more than 65,000 shareholders, mostly in Canada. Its majority shareholder at 69.6 percent is Standard Oil successor, Exxon Mobil Corporation.

Finally, Imperial Oil is a major stakeholder in the most famous name in the oil sands, Syncrude.

Alberta's oil deposits, particularly the oil sands, have always been a puzzle. The question is: what is the most efficient way to recover the maximum amount of oil?

Roger Butler, a British-born engineer who worked with Imperial Oil, the provincial government's Alberta Oil Sands Technology and Research Authority (AOSTRA) and the University of Calgary, invented the process now used by most oil sands operators to recover deep oil. Butler's invention is known as steam-assisted gravity drainage, or SAGD (pronounced "sag-dee") for short. Before he went into the oil patch, Butler worked in Saskatchewan potash mines, where water was injected underground to dissolve deposits to ease recovery.

After Imperial Oil made its mid-1960s discovery of a huge heavy oil deposit at Cold Lake, Butler recalled the injection process and wondered. The company transferred him in 1975 from Sarnia to Calgary, where he took up the oil sands problem with steam injection in mind. One well would pump in steam, which would soften the oil mixture, causing it to drain to the bottom. Another well would suck up the loosened material. Initially, the process couldn't produce enough to justify its costs. But then Butler realized that one horizontal well could create a series of drainage points, and his calculations suggested production of thousands of barrels per day.

At Cold Lake in 1978, Imperial Oil drilled the first well under Butler's theory. The horizontal well was about 150 metres long—today they're usually about 800 metres. "The oil came out at about the right rate— I felt pretty damn good," Butler told *Alberta Oil* magazine.

He took early retirement from Imperial Oil but worked at AOSTRA for about a year, further developing SAGD, and continued the research when he was appointed to the University of Calgary's first endowed chair in petroleum engineering.

Today, versions of SAGD are applied by most oil sands players. Only an estimated 10 percent of the oil sands were accessible under surface methods developed by Karl Clark. Butler's SAGD invention opened an estimated 90 percent of the oil sands to development. Butler, who died in 2005 in his late 70s, had introduced a method that would free up billions of dollars, perhaps trillions, in oil sands revenue.

In July 2006, the Canadian Petroleum Hall of Fame Society named Butler among eight new inductees.

Bitumania

Ken Jamieson went from a childhood on the Alberta prairie to the highest post in the boardroom of the world's biggest corporation, Exxon. Jamieson, whose father lived to be the oldest veteran of the North West Mounted Police, was born in Medicine Hat in 1910. He attended the University of Alberta before transferring to engineering at the Massachusetts Institute of Technology. After struggling through the Depression, Jamieson took a labour position at a Calgary refinery and began working his way up. During World War II, he served as oil liaison officer between Canada and the U.S. and was later picked up by Imperial Oil, then Standard Oil of New Jersey. He became president of Standard's Latin American subsidiaries and later brought about significant streamlining at subsidiary Humble Oil. He took U.S. citizenship in 1964 and was appointed Standard (later renamed Exxon) president in 1965. By 1969, he was chairman and CEO, positions he held until 1975. He quit the board in 1981.

CHAPTER TWENTY-TWO

Syncrude
A Consortium of Energy Companies Launches an Oil Sands Giant

THE BIGGEST NAME IN THE OIL SANDS GAME IS SYNCRUDE, YET Albertans and investors cannot find a profit (or loss) statement for the massive operation. That's because Syncrude is not a single entity, but a consortium of companies, each reporting its financial statements separately. But that doesn't mean that Syncrude doesn't want Albertans to understand its importance to their economy.

"Last year, for example, our economic contribution to Alberta came in at about $4.1 billion," Jim Carter, Syncrude president and chief operating officer, told an Edmonton economic conference in the spring of 2006. "That includes things like royalties and payroll taxes, salaries and benefits. But the biggest chunk typically comes from the procurement of goods and services, which, in 2005, totalled $2.9 billion. And the bulk of it, $1.4 billion, was spent right here in Edmonton, and a similar amount was spent in the Fort McMurray area."

Imperial Oil, Gulf Canada, Atlantic Richfield Canada and Canada-Cities Service—all U.S.-controlled firms—formed the Syncrude consortium in the early 1960s to apply to the province for a massive oil sands plant. Frank Spragins of Imperial Oil was named Syncrude president. He warned that delays could put oil sands development on a backburner because American investors might put their money elsewhere, such as the development of oil shale deposits in Colorado. Conversely, Canada's conventional oil developers, the companies that simply drilled holes and pumped out oil and gas, considered the oil sands a difficult competitor. They argued that provincial policy changes would result in more investment flowing to the oil sands and less to the search for conventional oil. As a result of these kinds of arguments, Suncor predecessor Great Canadian Oil Sands (GCOS) was operating at the time under a provincial policy that prohibited direct competition. There was only room for one player. In 1966, Premier Ernest Manning met with oil industry officials to discuss policy changes. Bickering went on for two years. However, Manning realized that U.S. demand for oil was going to grow, and establishing productive oil sands operations would confirm Alberta's position as a stable supplier.

The province brought in a new oil sands policy, and that same year, 1968, the Syncrude group renewed its application. It took another year for the Syncrude plan to pass through hearings and the approval process. Alberta's regulating conservation board, now called the Alberta Energy and Utilities Board, approved the project in 1969.

Things changed again in August 1971, when Alberta voters dumped the long-running Social Credit government in favour of the Progressive Conservatives led by Peter Lougheed. It took until 1973—the height of the world energy crisis and Lougheed's battle with Ottawa over control of natural resource revenue—for Syncrude to reach a royalty agreement with the province. But with approval and an agreement in place, the project was finally ready to launch construction in the spring of 1974. For Lougheed, Syncrude fit right in with his overall political strategy of building Alberta into more than just an oil economy. Syncrude would create thousands of jobs; maintain an oil industry as conventional supplies diminished; and foster engineering, management and fiscal expertise.

In 1974, Atlantic Richfield pulled out of the consortium to concentrate on Alaskan projects, but also because the initial $960-million Syncrude project cost had ballooned to $2.2 billion. It was the first of many ownership changes for Syncrude. However, the Atlantic Richfield move came at a critical time, placing the entire project in jeopardy. Syncrude and the province went searching for new investors. The new group included Imperial Oil, Cities Service, Gulf, the provinces of Alberta and Ontario and the federal government.

Syncrude officially opened in 1978. But, repeating what Suncor and the smaller pioneers had already learned, the cost of production was high. During a 1978 tour, Saudi Arabia's oil minister, Sheik Ahmed Zaki Yamani, was told that Syncrude spent between US$15 and US$20 to produce a barrel of oil. World prices were about US$19 per barrel.

"It costs us 40 cents a barrel," Yamani said.

But Syncrude proved to be the moneymaker the province had hoped and planned for, even with fluctuations in world oil prices. Despite its difficulties, Syncrude went ahead in 1983 with a $12-billion expansion plan, aimed at increasing production from 100,000 barrels a day to 130,000 barrels a day.

In 1989, Syncrude promoted vice-president Eric Newell, another former Imperial Oil manager, to CEO.

"In those days, the original vision of Syncrude was like a typical mining project," said Newell. "It was designed to run for 25 years. Startup was 1978, so the expectation was it would be mined by 2003, and in that period of time, it would have produced a billion barrels of oil, and would have generated about a billion dollars in royalties for the government." With Newell at the helm, Syncrude went far beyond any initial hopes and plans. (As did many other oil sands ventures.)

"We didn't have the technology to build farther out or to bring bitumen in," recalled Newell. "We have an annual R&D seminar. It was at those that our guys laid out where we were and where we had to go. And that was remote satellite mines, where bitumen could be sent to a central upgrader."

Gradually, understanding of the oil sands improved and so did the extraction processes. Earlier plants were small operations that treated bitumen captured at locations nearby, easily transported by conveyer belt or hauled by small trucks. Now, the plan was to establish one large upgrading facility and to bring bitumen from locations throughout the region into that central facility.

"The extraction process was so energy intensive," said Newell. "One of the keys to go to remote satellite mining would be to learn how to extract bitumen at a lot lower temperatures. From there, very systematically, we went about developing all the technology platforms that ultimately got us to the Aurora mine." Aurora is a new bitumen mine site and is part of the $8.4 billion Syncrude 21 expansion project, officially completed in 2006. The new mine uses an extraction system operating at 50°C rather than the 80°C required by earlier technology. The expansion also brought in a "hydrotransport" system, technology developed by Syncrude to transport oil sand slurry by pipeline from mine to extraction plant. While moving through the hydrotransporter, the bitumen is churned up, creating mechanical energy.

"We went from driveline bucketwheel and conveyer belt with extraction at 80°C—you know, using the old Clark hot-water process—to large trucks, shovels and hydrotransport key enabling technology," Newell happily boasts. "The key thing was the hot-water extraction process. You've got sand with a little bit of water around it and then the bitumen. So what you're trying to do is to break that bond. If you do that, the sand will fall to the bottom, and the bitumen will rise. Clark did that through his washing machine. We said, okay, can we replace that thermal energy and do the same thing with mechanical energy? They found if you put it in a slurry and ran it over a number of kilometres, you've got enough mechanical energy that it actually broke the water bond."

With the processes improving, Syncrude produced its one billionth barrel five years ahead of schedule, Newell said.

"The government really liked us because by that time they had $3 billion in royalties, and the best news of all was that we wouldn't be shutting down. We had the technology, in fact, to expand production and move forward."

In the early 1990s, Newell became one of the driving forces behind the National Task Force on Oil Sands, which resulted in a series of initiatives that opened Athabasca to incredible investment by smoothing regulatory and royalty concerns.

Syncrude was one of the first companies out of the gate. It announced the Syncrude 21 project in the mid-1990s and launched Stage One—a de-bottlenecking and mine expansion—in 1996, moving on to two further stages, including an upgrader expansion between 2001 and 2006.

Newell also brought in new commitments to environmental standards and provided training and employment to aboriginal peoples of the region. Syncrude spent millions on its promises to Native people and environmental issues. Among the initiatives was a land reclamation project for a mined area. Although it could not replace muskeg, the company seeded the area to provide grassland for wood bison. In 1993, Syncrude, under Newell, set up a bison cooperative project with the Fort MacKay First Nation.

"The path we've taken over the last 10 years—indeed, since we started up in 1978—has been almost as well planned and as carefully charted and managed as a mission to the moon," said Jim Carter. "Stage Three, including the expansion of our upgrader, will increase our production capacity to 350,000 barrels of crude oil a day. It was also one of the largest industrial projects of its kind in the world."

Syncrude has more than 20 active Canadian and U.S. patents and is ranked among Canada's top research firms. Total research spending is about $40 million to $50 million per year.

Syncrude may not report profits or losses publicly, but it does release an annual public statement that gives limited production and financial details. For 2005, Syncrude stated 214,000 barrels per day production at an average cost of $26.59 per barrel. The previous year's cost per barrel was $18.61. Syncrude attributed the increased per-barrel costs to higher input prices, such as natural gas.

Bitumania

The Syncrude Consortium in 1975

Imperial Oil Ltd.	31.25 percent
Cities Service	22 percent
Gulf Canada	16.75 percent
Federal government	15 percent
Alberta government	10 percent
Ontario government	5 percent

The Syncrude Consortium in 2006

Canadian Oil Sands Ltd.	31.74 percent
Imperial Oil Ltd.	25 percent
Petro-Canada Oil and Gas	12 percent
Conoco Phillips Oil Sands Partnership II	9.03 percent
Nexen Oil Sands Partnership	7.23 percent
Canadian Oil Sands Limited Partnership	5 percent
Mocal Energy Ltd.	5 percent
Murphy Oil Company Ltd.	5 percent

CHAPTER TWENTY-THREE

The National Energy Program
A Federal Initiative Enrages Alberta Oil Producers

BICKERING BETWEEN ALBERTA AND OTTAWA ERUPTED INTO ALL-OUT political war in the early 1980s, when the federal government introduced the National Energy Program (NEP).

Announced in Pierre Trudeau's October 1980 budget, the NEP sparked angry protests, killed jobs and trimmed billions from the Alberta economy. To this day, serious concern flares in Alberta when any federal move remotely suggests action similar to the NEP, such as a carbon tax.

The program was designed to share energy wealth across the country and establish energy self-sufficiency by 1990. Sounds good, but it just didn't work, and there were plenty of reasons why.

The Trudeau Liberals returned to power in February 1980, ousting the short-lived Joe Clark Tories. During the campaign, Trudeau made an issue of energy policy, including hints of federal action. His talk caught Lougheed's attention. The Conservative Alberta premier braced for another battle like the one in 1973–74, but he couldn't have known what was about to hit him.

The Trudeau election was followed in May by the first Québec referendum, in which 59.6 percent of Québecers voted to remain part of Canada. Trudeau took that vote as a victory and turned his attention to the dithering economy.

"The government of Canada and its ministers are elected to seek the good of the whole country, so sometimes that means saying no to one region and yes to another in order to redistribute equality of opportunity," Trudeau said. Alberta's resource wealth was clearly in target.

The world energy crisis had driven up the price of crude and gas significantly. Pricing talks between Alberta and Ottawa dragged on without resolution. Trudeau's trusted colleague, Energy Minister Marc Lalonde, spent the rest of the year preparing the new national strategy, without consulting either the provinces or the oil industry. Twenty-five years later, Lalonde told the *Calgary Sun* there was no point trying to reason with Alberta.

"We tried to work out some kind of a deal whereby our objectives would be achieved, but they didn't want to hear about it, they wouldn't budge," said Lalonde. "It was clear that we would not be able to work out a deal unless we staked our ground quite firmly and clearly." When the NEP was introduced in the House, Lalonde said it was only fair for Canadians to seize control of energy resources. The new program was designed to drastically increase revenue to the federal government.

It hit Alberta like a bomb.

NEP terms included:

- bringing in new taxes on oil and gas;
- limiting foreign ownership by restricting permits for production to companies with at least 50 percent Canadian ownership;

- establishing grants and subsidies under a "Petroleum Incentives Program" (amounts available were based on percentage of Canadian ownership);
- a requirement for all producers to purchase Canadian goods and services;
- a special tax to help Ottawa buy out foreign-owned firms;
- reserving a 25 percent Crown interest on current and future leases;
- incentive grants to drill in remote areas.

Also included was a "made in Canada" oil price.

The NEP document stated that energy revenue shares to each government evolved over time: "The result is a distribution of benefits that is extraordinarily unfavourable to the national government.... There must be recognition of a national claim—a claim by all Canadians—to a share in these revenues and benefits."

The program met with general approval in Eastern Canada, where consumers were suspicious of "Big Oil" and simply considered Alberta greedy. But industry signalled the market reaction. In the following few days, the Toronto Stock Exchange oil and gas index plummeted 800 points. Brokers sold so many oil and gas shares that trading in many companies was suspended.

Two days after the federal budget address announcing the NEP, Lougheed made a 27-minute radio and TV address that is now part of Alberta lore.

"The Ottawa government has without negotiation, without agreement, simply walked into our home and occupied the living room," Lougheed said.

The angry premier outlined a counter attack that included cutting Alberta oil production. Cuts were planned in three stages at three-month intervals and, when completed, would curb production by 180,000 barrels a day—the equivalent of 10 percent of Canadian consumption. The move would cost Ottawa millions of dollars a day in lost revenue, and it would have to make up the difference in supply through imports.

"It was an attack on Alberta, so there was no way other than for me to go on province-wide television and explain to our citizens what had happened and how damaging it was and how we would fight back and work our way through," Lougheed told the *Calgary Sun*. "It was extremely dramatic for us to take the position that we're reducing the amount of essential commodity oil to the rest of Canada.... I think if we hadn't been that dramatic and that strong, we wouldn't have made the settlement that we had to make."

Lalonde told the *Calgary Sun* there "would not have been a big fuss" about the NEP if energy prices had remained high. But they didn't. Prices began falling as a result of a world oil glut.

Canadian Hunter Exploration co-founder Jim Gray branded the NEP a "determined attack" on the oil industry. "We were finally getting our legs," Gray said in the *Calgary Sun*. "We were developing confidence in the late 1970s. Here we were, finally starting to stand on our own feet and big mother Ottawa came and struck us down. We were upset, disappointed; we were mad; we were all those things. When it hit on October 28, it came as a really devastating blow, and I think the thing that surprised everyone was how quickly the industry turned down."

Alberta unemployment doubled in the year following the NEP announcement. It tripled between 1981 and 1983.

Housing starts, a major contributor to any economy in terms of investment and jobs, stalled. Drilling levels tapered off, becoming negligible, and major projects were shelved.

"I was just horrified," John Masters, Gray's Canadian Hunter co-founder, said in the *Calgary Sun* series. "Those were the days when there were 10-mile-long lines of drilling rigs stopped at the border before they left Canada for the United States. And those of us in Calgary just, quite legitimately I think, just hated that Liberal government in Ottawa at the time, and I guess they hated us."

Masters soon found himself in a public screaming match with Lalonde. Masters described the NEP with words such as "disreputable," "criminal" and even "Nazi-like." Unimpressed, Lalonde fired back, saying that Masters, who was born in Oklahoma, made millions at the expense of Canadians and never bothered to take citizenship.

"I think the bastards tried to damage us just about as much as they could," said Masters. "I was just so pissed off with those guys I would've fought with any one of them on the street corner." The tirade won him admiration from fellow Albertans, including an incident in which Masters and his wife were greeted with applause as they entered a Calgary restaurant.

American reaction was delayed because the NEP was announced just days before a presidential election that brought in Ronald Reagan. But once organized, the U.S. took its typical free-market stance. The Americans argued that regulated pricing would not achieve self-sufficiency, and Canadian consumers would become dependent on the government for energy subsidy. Obviously, the U.S. took its strongest objection to the NEP actions that limited foreign corporations. In retaliation, the U.S. threatened changes to the Auto Pact and hinted at restrictions on Canadian corporate activity in the U.S.

Lougheed's threat did not produce immediate results. Months went by with no progress by either side. By March 1981, nothing had changed, and Lougheed was forced to implement the first cutback of 60,000 barrels a day. The federal government simply implemented a 75-cent per barrel levy to cover the increased cost of importing crude. By June 1, Lougheed had to impose a second cut. As the deadline approached for the final cut on September 1, the two sides at last negotiated a deal. The five-year pact ended the Lougheed cutbacks and brought in a series of price increases, moving the Canadian price closer to world prices.

"It was clearly a federal budget that was used by Mr. Lalonde and his cohorts to try to take the resource revenues and change the constitution of Canada. There wasn't any real negotiation," said Lougheed 25 years after the NEP. "It's hard to think of anything else in the 100-year history of our province that was as dramatic as that, where the federal government challenged the rights of Albertans."

Killing the NEP was one of the first moves of the Brian Mulroney Tory government.

Bitumania

In-situ production relies on horizontal drilling, a technology that developed in the 1980s and became more widely available in the 1990s. After reaching the desired depth vertically in conventional drilling, a motor is lowered to operate flexible tubing with drill bits that can be steered using data transmitted to the surface operator. Horizontal drilling can then make a wide sweep of the underground reservoir.

CHAPTER TWENTY-FOUR

Big Oil
Some Names Have Been Around a Long Time, Others are Moving In

OILMEN SELL COMPANIES LIKE THEY SELL THE PRODUCT OUT OF THE ground. Over the years, oil companies have come and gone, and being a big fish in the pond doesn't always guarantee survival, as the Dome story reveals. Here's a look at some who have thrived, and some of the huge foreign-based multinational companies that are making their way into Alberta, particularly the oil sands.

Petro-Canada
A 1968 federal report on industry showed that foreign companies, or partially foreign-owned companies, held 99 percent of Canada's refining and marketing capacity, 65 percent of oil and gas production and 95 percent of petrochemicals. Although the report was from a left-leaning author, the Trudeau government got the message and undertook initiatives to put more Canadian ownership into industry. In the energy sector, the call for more home control became acute with the OPEC energy crisis of the early 1970s. Thus, in 1975, legislation was introduced to create Crown corporation Petro-Canada. It began operations at a Calgary hotel on January 1, 1976, with two assets: 45 percent of Panarctic Oils and 15 percent of the Syncrude joint venture project, which was under construction.

Petro-Canada's first chairman was Maurice Strong, who had worked under Jack Gallagher at Dome and for politically powerful Canadian billionaire Paul Desmarais of Power Corp. Former Imperial Oil geologist Wilbert "Bill" Hopper became president. Hopper had travelled the globe as a petroleum consultant before settling into a civil service career at the federal energy, mines and resources department. Before he died in 2006, former federal Energy Minister Marc Lalonde praised Hopper's work at Petro-Canada and credited him for the Crown corporation's impressive growth.

Hopper stayed in Ottawa and commuted by corporate jet to Calgary weekly. He got busy and created new cash flow by buying into existing East Coast operations and then acquiring Atlantic Richfield assets for about $342 million, which the Calgary oil elite considered a steal. "These guys would do business with Chairman Mao if his money was green," Hopper responded, referring to the communist Chinese leader.

Hopper then lost an attempt to take over Husky Oil, but went after Oklahoma-based Phillips Petroleum's controlling shares in Frank McMahon's Pacific Petroleums and Westcoast Transmission. Strong left Petro-Canada in 1978, but Hopper, who had advanced to CEO, continued the expansion drive. After gaining controlling interest of Pacific Petroleums and Westcoast Transmission in 1979, Petro-Canada then completed the takeover through a tender offer for the remaining shares. The total cost of the deal came to $1.5 billion, but Petro-Canada was now an integrated national oil company with production, refining, retail service stations and pipelines. Suddenly, a company that had started with two guys, a typewriter and cab fare had more than $3 billion in assets, second only in Canada to Imperial Oil. The company built huge headquarters in Calgary with imported red granite, inspiring critics and fed-bashers to dub it "Red Square." Anti-government resentment seethed, as indicated in a new popular bumper sticker: "I'd rather push this car a mile than fill up at Petro-Canada." Yet the company continued on its course. Also in 1979, Petro-Canada's East Coast interests made the huge offshore Hibernia discovery, as well as gas finds off Nova Scotia.

In 1981, Petro-Canada picked up Petrofina Canada for $1.6 billion and then BP Canada in 1983, followed by a $900-million acquisition of Gulf Canada's refineries and service stations in 1985.

When the federal government switched to the Brian Mulroney Tories in 1984, there came the inevitable Conservative push to get government out of business. The feds instructed Petro-Canada to change its mandate, operate like a private business and concentrate on profits. By 1990, Mulroney's government was preparing privatization legislation for Petro-Canada, and though it kept 70 percent of the shares, the oil company sold public shares on the stock exchange on July 3, 1991. Then, in 1995, the government further reduced its share holding to 20 percent.

In the boardroom, Hopper was starting to lose support, and he was fired in 1993. The two people who had started Petro-Canada in a hotel room discussing potential takeover targets and growth were both gone.

Petro-Canada soon stretched out beyond Canadian borders, finding oil in Algeria in 1994. Today it has operations in Europe, Africa and Latin America.

The federal government began hinting at a final selloff of its Petro-Canada shares in 2004. The sale, the largest public share offering in Canadian history, was completed in late September that year. About 49.4 million shares sold at $64.50 each, fetching $3.2 billion for the federal government.

"It was a blockbuster transaction, and it went absolutely like clockwork and produced a highly desirable result for Canadian taxpayers," federal Finance Minister Ralph Goodale told media. The sale came as oil prices were soaring and investors were clamouring to buy energy stocks. "Is there an element of good luck in that? I think there probably was. But the fact of the matter is good management also tends to generate its own good luck," said Goodale. Although the federal government relinquished ownership, laws still require Petro-Canada to limit anyone from owning more than 20 percent and to keep its head office in Calgary.

Petro-Canada's major operations remain at home, in Canada. The company announced its tuned-up oil sands strategy in 2003, and by 2005, it had picked up a 60 percent interest in UTS Energy Corp.'s Fort Hills oil sands project for $300 million. The project's total cost could be as much as $5 billion. Later that year, the partners brought in Teck Cominco to help share costs. The Fort Hills project will include a new upgrader, with Sturgeon County, just north of Edmonton, as the likely location.

Petro-Canada reported 2005 net earnings of $1.791 billion on $17.585 billion revenues (net earnings included $115 million from oil sands). That compared to $1.757 billion net earnings for 2004 on revenues of $14.27 billion. The company has 5000 employees.

EnCana
After weeks of rumours, in January 2002, two of Canada's biggest oil and gas companies held a joint press conference to announce a blockbuster merger. Bringing

the Alberta Energy Company (AEC) and PanCanadian Energy together would create a behemoth with $27 billion in market capitalization and good assets around the world. The proposed name of the new firm was EnCana Corp.

"We're talking about one of the highest-growth companies—if not the highest-growth company—in the business," said Gwyn Morgan, AEC chief executive officer and designated boss for EnCana. Between them, PanCanadian and AEC had assets off Nova Scotia and in the North Sea, Gulf of Mexico, Latin America and the Alberta oil sands.

"As the energy business becomes more capital intensive and more international in nature, size and scale become important determinants of corporate competitiveness and success," said David O'Brien, PanCanadian's CEO. It was another way of saying that getting bigger made it tougher for some other company to buy them out. Alberta's oil patch had recently had a spate of U.S. acquisitions, particularly big purchases by giants Anadarko Petroleum Corp. (which bought Berkley Petroleum and Gulfstream Resources), Conoco (purchased Gulf Canada Resources), Burlington Resources (took over Canadian Hunter) and Hunt Oil (gained Chieftain International). Some commentators suggested that EnCana was so big, only a handful of companies in the world—Exxon, Royal Dutch, Total, or BP Amoco—could afford a hostile takeover bid. By the same token, the sheer size of the new corporation was enough to put its shares on the radar screen for a wider range of small U.S. investors and others around the world.

By early April, regulators and shareholders had given approval—EnCana was a go. The new company's roots went back more than 100 years, to when Canadian Pacific Rail was pushing through the West and sent out a few drilling crews to find water. Near Medicine Hat, they found natural gas instead. The CPR set up the Canadian Pacific Oil and Gas Company in 1958 to focus on diversifying into resources development. The CPR was looking for assets throughout western Canada and found Central-Del Rio Oils, which had taken leases from the rail company and had promising leads in Alberta and Saskatchewan. The CPR bought 52 percent of Central-Del Rio on the open market, then negotiated a merger in 1971. The new firm was named PanCanadian Petroleum.

That was about four years before the Peter Lougheed government created the Alberta Energy Company as a provincial crown corporation. The AEC was half owned by the province and the other half of the shares went to the public, raising $273 million. Its main asset was oil and gas rights in the Suffield military range, but the province also gave AEC a contract to operate the Syncrude power plant and pipelines. The AEC had an option for a 20 percent ownership of Syncrude and eventually took a 13.75 percent stake.

By the turn of the 21st century, PanCanadian and AEC were the largest Canadian-owned oil and gas producers.

Over time, the province gradually sold off bits of AEC until Premier Ralph Klein, on a tear to clear the province's debt, sold the remainder in 1994 for $500 million. AEC's 20-year run as a crown corporation was over. PanCanadian's status would soon change as well.

The CPR subsidiary suddenly found its independence in 2001, when Canadian Pacific broke its mining, hotel, forestry, shipping and energy units into free-standing companies. Soon, Gwyn Morgan came knocking at PanCanadian's door.

On April 8, 2002, accompanied by Canadian superstar figure skaters David Pelletier and Jamie Sale, new EnCana chairman David O'Brien visited the New York Stock Exchange, where the new company's shares shot up five percent on the first day of trading.

For the 2005 fiscal year, EnCana, which reports in U.S. dollars, had a cash flow of US$7.426 billion on net earnings of US$3.426 billion.

Shell Canada

Shell Canada Ltd. is a 60 percent partner in the massive Athabasca Oil Sands Project (AOSP), which includes the Muskeg River mine, 75 kilometres north of Fort McMurray, and the Scotford upgrader near Edmonton. Related to the project is the Corridor pipeline that connects the two. The $1.4-billion mine and its $1.9-billion upgrader were approved in 1999, and the $500 million pipeline shortly thereafter. The mine was expected to reach production of 150,000 barrels a day by 2002. It's operated by Albian Sands Energy Inc., which Shell says is appropriately named after the ancient seabed buried under Athabasca and the source of the oil sands. By 2001, Shell and project partners Chevron Canada and Western Oil Sands, with 20 percent each, were forced to admit the project would come in at closer to $5.2 billion because of higher labour and construction costs. Costs skyrocketed because demand outstripped supply in the oil sands blitz. (Shell wasn't the only company in the oil sands with severe overruns—Suncor's Millennium and Syncrude's 21 suffered as well.)

Shell Canada says that, at full capacity, AOSP supplies 10 percent of Canada's oil needs.

Yet, in July 2006, the AOSP partners prepared to embark on a 100,000-barrel-a-day addition that would require between 6000 and 7000 construction workers at its peak. Cost of the expansion, originally planned at about $4 billion when AOSP opened in 2003, was readjusted to between $10 billion and $12.8 billion. Shell Canada President Clive Mather said the expansion plan includes a contingency allowance for rising materials and labour costs that could not be predicted.

"A very similar position exists right around the world wherever you're looking at developing resources today," Mather said at a press conference. "This is a high-quality resource in an area of very low risk. Compared to any of the alternatives, Alberta is still a great place to invest."

Mather outlined a long-range oil sands strategy—still in development—including further expansion at Athabasca, possible in-situ extraction at Peace River and Cold Lake, plus integration of new upgraders or refineries. Shell Canada eventually hopes to ramp up its total Athabasca production, including the yet-to-launch $2-billion Jackpine project, to 550,000 barrels per day.

It shouldn't be surprising that Shell is one of the biggest operators in the oil sands, or in Alberta for that matter, because the company has been around just about as long as Imperial Oil.

Parent company Royal Dutch Shell was originally a Dutch and British partnership, operating from Russia to Indonesia with a bigger fleet than the British Navy. The company was among the Seven Sisters, the biggest of the early oil companies that together dominated world operations from the 1911 breakup of Standard Oil into 34 other companies until the 1970s rise of OPEC's new-found power.

Royal Dutch Shell incorporated Shell Company of Canada in 1911 with the equivalent of about $1 million today.

However, the British Admiralty took over the Montréal plant during wartime and didn't return control until 1921. Operations expanded to include service stations, bulk fuel plants and refineries in BC and Montréal. The company moved its head office to Toronto in 1930. Exploration in Western Canada began with Shell Oil Co. of New York when it opened a Calgary office in 1939. The company made its first Alberta natural gas discovery at Jumping Pound in 1944.

Shell missed out on Leduc No. 1, the most famous oil strike ever in Alberta. Carl Nickle of *Nickle's Daily Oil Bulletin* called it "the worst move in the history of the Canadian oil patch." Nickle reports that Shell also dropped deals in the Redwater fields.

During World War II, Shell acted as a major supplier to Canada and Britain. After the war, the company was careful about getting back into exploration and decided to concentrate on areas that were more likely to produce rather than on untested, unlikely zones such as Leduc. It gave up all its Canadian properties to concentrate on Venezuela. To re-establish itself in Western Canada, Shell set off on a series of acquisitions. By 1957, Shell Company of Canada had bought out its American sister. The company went on to take up North Star Oil and its 1000 service stations and a Manitoba refinery in 1961, and Canadian Oil with its 2900 stations and two refineries in 1962. It became Shell Canada Ltd. in 1963.

Shell's first attempt at the oil sands came with the takeover of Canadian Oils, a partner in the proposed Great Canadian Oil Sands project. But Shell and Canadian Pacific pulled out before GCOS started, citing concerns over provincial politics, royalties, federal sales taxes and a consultant's report that warned it might take 10 years to reach profitability.

After putting the oil sands on the shelf for a time, Shell was back at it in the early 1970s with the formation of the Alsands consortium. The cost of the proposed 137,000-barrel-a-day project was pegged at $5.1 billion, and though Shell considered going it alone, the company found it wiser to seek partners. The consortium came together with Amoco, Chevron, Dome, Gulf, Hudson's Bay Oil and Gas Co., Pacific Petroleums and PetroFina. By then, OPEC had changed world energy projects. Synthetic projects were only viable if world prices were high. With reduced incentives available from both governments and a low world price, Imperial delayed its Cold Lake heavy-oil project and Syncrude put expansion on hold. By 1982, the Alsands proposal was dead. The Alsands collapse came as a hard blow to the Lougheed government, which was struggling to get more oil sands development moving.

The AOSP got on track in August 1999, when Western Oil Sands Inc. and Chevron Canada Resources Ltd. each bought a 20 percent stake to partner with Shell. "It wasn't a matter of if we would get a partner, but when," Neil Camarta, Shell's vice-president of oil sands told reporters.

Husky
Husky Energy's fortunes began in a small American town, but today rest in the hands of a Hong Kong billionaire.

The company was founded in 1938 in Cody, Wyoming, by devout Mormon Glenn Nielson, who built up the Husky Refining Company from one small refinery with 19 employees. In a bid to capitalize on heavy oil and asphalt opportunities in Canada, Husky moved its refining in 1946 to Lloydminster, Alberta, with a wholly owned subsidiary headquartered in Calgary. It took substantial heavy oil holdings in the area; holdings that became attractive to other companies. By 1952, the company had issued shares, surpassed its U.S. parent and, in fact, picked up all out-standing shares in the American firm.

A bidding war broke out in the early summer of 1978. On June 8 that year, Husky's shares rocketed from $4.75 to $35.75 on rumours that it was a takeover target. Husky had already been wooed by both Petro-Canada and Gulf Canada, but spurned them both. Now Petro-Canada was making an unsolicited bid of $45 per share, valuing the company at $490 million. "I felt that I had a gun at my head and a gun at my back," Nielson told *Blue-Eyed Sheiks* author Peter Foster.

Nielson immediately set out to find a white knight before Petro-Canada could exercise its offer. Husky was able to start a bidding war been Petro-Canada and Occi-dental Petroleum Corp. of California. Occidental bid, Petro-Canada topped it and Occidental went even higher, to $54 per share. Quietly, in the background, Alberta Gas Trunk Line (AGTL) under President Bob Blair was buy-ing Husky shares. Blair had initially bought the shares as an investment, but a little research showed that going for minority control could be more lucrative. By Friday, June 23, AGTL had bought up to 10 percent of Husky, and by the following Monday, he shored up 23 percent, then 35 percent by Tuesday. Blair suddenly quit buying—and Husky's shares plummeted.

After the dust settled, AGTL agreed in 1979 to buy out Nielson's shares for $48 each. In 1984, the U.S. subsidiary was sold off, and that was followed by a 1987 reorganization in which Nova Corp. (formerly AGTL) and Hutchison Whampoa of Hong Kong took the company private. That deal raised the usual media and political worries that foreign interests were taking over Canada's energy industry. Blair said he met Hong Kong billionaire Li Ka-shing, head and

major stakeholder in Hutchison Whampoa, four years earlier while AGTL was doing some engineering work for
Husky in Hong Kong. The deal brought Husky $484 mil-
lion, but it cost the company a 43 percent equity stake,
taken by Hutchison Whampoa.

By 1991, Nova had debt problems of its own and will-
ingly sold its remaining Husky stake to the Li-controlled
interests. Li's son Victor is co-chairman today. Husky
strengthened its position in a number of areas, including
the acquisition of Mohawk gas stations in 1998, the same
year it bought out Saskatchewan's stake in the bi-provincial
upgrader at Lloydminster. Initially a joint project between
Husky, Alberta, Saskatchewan and the federal government,
the upgrader was completed in 1992 for $1.6 billion. Husky
and the government of Saskatchewan became 50-50 partners in 1995, buying out Alberta and the feds. By 1998,
Husky had bought out Saskatchewan for sole ownership.

In August 2006, Husky announced completion of its
$500-million Tucker Lake oil sands project in Athabasca
and said it was planning a $2.3 billion expansion at the
Lloydminster upgrader, which is expected to handle oil
from Tucker Lake.

Husky is also active in offshore development in Eastern
Canada. Today, Husky Energy has about $16 billion in
assets, 4000 employees and reported earnings in 2005 of
$2 billion, which was double from the previous year.

ATCO

Calgary fireman Samuel Donald Southern and his son
Ron put up $4000 in 1946 to launch the Alberta Trailer
Hire Company, renting two-wheel trailers to the city.
The Leduc oil discovery in 1947 greatly increased demand
for mobile housing, and the elder Southern expanded his

small business to meet the new market. In 1951, the company was incorporated as Alberta Trailer Company, which is today ATCO.

Son Ron completed a bachelor of science degree at the University of Alberta and took over the company in 1956 while his father sat as chairman.

"Prior to ATCO coming along, if you wanted to house people in temporary areas, you either put them in tents or you built a town," Ron Southern told *Alberta Report* in 1995. "We decided to build something portable, strong and warm. And in doing so, we created a whole new industry for the world."

A manufacturing plant and partnership called Roadway Industries opened in 1953 in Edmonton but was destroyed in a 1955 fire while it was working on its largest order yet, 68 units. The Roadway partnership dissolved, and ATCO re-established manufacturing at Airdrie.

ATCO trailers became a common sight at rig and forestry sites throughout remote areas.

By 1962, the expanding company was re-incorporated as ATCO Industries, with plants in Canada, the U.S. and Australia, and began diversifying into other areas, first supplying trailers to hospitals, schools and offices, then moving into oil and gas development. Among ATCO's acquisitions was Canadian Utilities of Edmonton, a natural gas and electricity distributor. The company went public in 1968.

Subsidiary ATCO Gas & Oil Ltd. discovered oil in 1973, and by 1976, ATCO had $200 million in annual revenue.

The elder Southern died in 1990, but a new generation was waiting in the wings. By 2000, Ron Southern was co-CEO along with daughter Nancy Southern. Nancy has since graduated to president and CEO, while her father serves as chairman.

Ron and Marg Southern established Spruce Meadows, a show-jumping training ground near Calgary, in 1975. Originally, the Southerns imagined a junior training ground, so that equestrians such as their daughter didn't have to go elsewhere to compete. But Spruce Meadows evolved into a world-class facility, hosting major events. It has been ranked among the best in the world and has produced some of Canada's finest riders.

Today, ATCO Group has about 7000 employees and $7.5 billion in assets, including utilities, power generation, pipelines, facilities management, travel, noise management and billing services. In 2005, revenues were $2.859 billion.

Total

Paris-based Total SA subsidiary Total E&P Canada Ltd. completed a $1.58-billion takeover of Deer Creek Energy Ltd. and its Joslyn oil sands project in 2005. Then Total outlined plans for approximately $10.6 billion in capital expenditure in Alberta over the next decade.

The takeover came during a spate of foreign entries into Alberta's oil scene, with some people questioning whether the province was selling out its birthright. Former Deer Creek CEO Glen Schmidt, speaking as an Albertan and not an oilman, told *Alberta Oil* magazine that he had no problem with foreign companies buying into the oil sands. "We're the beneficiary," said Schmidt. "They take the risk, invest billions of dollars, and when it reaches payout, we have a steady cash-flow stream that provides taxes, royalties and jobs for a long time."

Total came into Alberta with heavy oil experience. Its Sincor project in Venezuela produces 200,000 barrels per day and includes an upgrader. Total is counting on that technical know-how, honed on its 47 percent stake in Sincor, as it tackles the challenges in the Athabasca sands.

"The attractiveness we see in the Alberta oil sands is the magnitude of the resources," Jean-Luc Guiziou, president of Total E&P Canada, told *Alberta Oil* magazine. "They are very large resources, and yes, they are technically challenging. But with projects in two countries, we have resources that can contribute to our worldwide portfolio on a very long term. We opened an Alberta office in 1998 specifically to assess the value of the Athabasca oil sands."

Total SA, the world's fourth largest oil and gas producer, was founded in the early 1920s. It divides its operations into three major categories: upstream (exploration and production), downstream (trading, shipping, refining and marketing) and, finally, chemicals. Total has operations in more than 130 countries and 111,000 staff worldwide.

Shortly after opening its Alberta office, Total took a stake in the $1.4-billion SAGD Surmont project in 1999, when it was a Gulf Canada initiative (it is now ConocoPhillips). Surmont, about 60 kilometres southeast of Fort McMurray, is planned to reach 100,000 barrels a day by 2010.

Deer Creek's asset was an 86 percent stake in the Joslyn project, about 60 kilometres north of Fort McMurray, between two other major projects including Syncrude. Now 100 percent owned by Total, Joslyn will apply both SAGD and open-pit mining. The Joslyn deposit is estimated at two billion barrels over 30 years of production. In addition, Total is also considering building an upgrader in Alberta—

a massive project that is estimated at $5 billion for a capacity of 200,000 barrels a day.

Total's foray into Canada was driven primarily by the massive oil sands opportunity. But it also liked the government and regulatory system.

"The business environment in Canada, and Alberta particularly, is welcoming. I mean that the authorities—the government and the regulators—are knowledgeable and they listen to companies. We have a true collaboration," said Guiziou.

The Chinese

China National Offshore Oil Corp. (CNOOC) bought a 17 percent stake in MEGEnergy Inc. of Calgary in 2005 for $150 million. One of the world's largest petroleum firms, CNOOC hopes to capitalize on two million barrels of MEG holdings in Alberta's northeast.

Two months later, state-owned Sinopec, China's second largest petroleum firm, paid $105 million to acquire a 40 percent stake in the Northern Lights project with Synenco Energy Inc.

Jim Donnell, president of Synenco, told the *Edmonton Sun* that he wasn't expecting any criticism about taking a foreign partner. "We know this transaction is extremely good for both Alberta and Canada—any $4.5 billion capital deployment is good, creation of several thousand jobs is good, creation of 1000 operation jobs is good, and certainly, the project is good for global crude supply."

Also in 2005, PetroChina International Co. signed a preliminary agreement to buy half of all crude shipped via the Gateway project, a $4-billion oil pipeline being developed by Canada's Enbridge Inc.

Oil analysts believe the Chinese are carefully learning from their two oil sands assets before making further investments. However, they say, with China's inevitable need to meet a growing demand for oil, that investment is likely to come.

Bitumania

In 1988, the Brian Mulroney Tory federal government pledged $1.7 billion in funding for the Other Six Lease Operators (OSLO) project. OSLO was first proposed in 1981 by Imperial Oil, Petro-Canada, PanCanadian Petroleum, Canadian Occidental, Gulf Canada and the Province of Alberta, to build the third major oil sands operation, with production estimated at up to 77,000 barrels per day. Times were tough—unemployment was high, oil prices were low. Alberta's Don Getty government counted on OSLO to contribute to an economic revival, but the project was plagued by public and industry concern over government handouts to get it going and make it profitable. The Mulroney government pulled out in 1990. By 1992, the project was dead. The combined failures of the proposed Alsands and OSLO set back oil sands development.

CHAPTER TWENTY-FIVE

The National Task Force on Oil Sands

A Group of Stakeholders Unleashes a Black Gold Rush

A 2006 SURVEY BY THE CANADIAN ASSOCIATION OF PETROLEUM Producers estimated that companies planned to spend up to $81 billion on Alberta oil sands projects up to 2016. That didn't include the recently completed multi-billion-dollar Syncrude 21 and Suncor Millennium projects. There is so much happening in the oil sands that some observers have called it the largest construction project currently in North America. It's been almost 100 years since Sidney Ells first explored the Athabasca region, and his enthusiastic first steps were followed by almost 50 years of frustration and failure. Even Great Canadian Oil Sands, the first major operator, and Syncrude, the pride of Alberta, were tentative about growth. And then, in the late 1990s and past the turn of the century, oil sands development exploded. What happened? There were a series of factors, not the least of which was that world oil prices, hovering as low as $10 per barrel in the mid-1990s, rebounded steadily, touching all-time highs above US$78 per barrel in 2006. That makes expensive oil sands investment a little more than tolerable. In addition, oil sands operators were getting smarter, more productive and more efficient. But the real catalyst, the one that sparked a stampede to the Athabasca deposits, was government ratification of a new royalty regime.

The 1997 National Task Force on Oil Sands Strategies let the genie out of the bottle. Syncrude's Eric Newell headed the joint industry-government collaboration, first formed in 1991 by the Alberta Chamber of Resources.

"Eric gets a lot of credit for leading that," said Suncor's Rick George. "It was significant. It was a very big part of our decision to go with Millennium."

It is a detailed package, but in essence, the task force recommended a level playing field—the same deal for everyone.

"It was absolutely key that we had to have a regime that was fair to all parties," said George. "Before that came into effect, what happened was that on every major project you went in and negotiated your own separate deal with the government. That never felt right to anybody. You're always going, 'Geez, if I cut this deal, is the next guy coming in the door going to get a better deal?' It's a very competitive industry. These things were so big and financially risky, they needed special terms, government handouts—that's the way it was. You had a big project and you negotiated royalty and tax terms on a project-by-project basis. This scared the hell out of investors."

Newell recalls that failure to get things going in the oil sands made him look for answers.

"The one that did it for me was the Other Six," said Newell, referring to the derailed Other Six Lease Operators (OSLO) project. "It, too, went on the shelf. A few us at the Chamber of Resources office were discussing it. We said, 'We need to develop this treasure. We need a task force.'" The group turned to the Mining Association of Canada, looking to include the task force recommendation in its annual report to the federal government's energy and mines department.

"This isn't well known, but it was September 24, 1991, in Halifax, the first time they approved this recommendation for a national oil sands task force," said Newell. "Jake Epp was the minister at the time. I always admired him for this. He'd gone back to Ottawa, and I guess his staff warned him: 'Here they come again, Jake. Those oil sands guys are coming for more handouts.' Well, of course, it was the opposite. We realized government couldn't give handouts. We also knew industry wasn't investing in oil sands. We wanted to get everybody together to figure it out."

Newell even invited environmental groups to take part, but was turned down. About 35 organizations did join in, some 70 people in all. The task force produced its vision in 1995.

"You'll recall that there were zero dollars of investment going into big oil sands projects," said Newell. "We have the technology planned, remote satellite mining, SAGD. Syncrude, Suncor and Imperial at Cold Lake were all doing a good job of getting costs under control. And we laid out this vision where we could triple oil sands production.

"We thought it would take us 25 years, and it would take $21 billion to $25 billion worth of projects. I can tell you, a lot of people thought we were smoking something funny. It's interesting. By 2005, less than 10 years later, we'd beaten all those goals. We'd tripled production. We'd gone over a million barrels per day. The industry had invested $34 billion in big projects, and the good news is that there was another $45 billion projected in the next seven or eight years.

"We got the terms right, the conditions right, and it was amazing how fast it took off."

The existing players, including Syncrude, Suncor and Imperial Oil, negotiated transition agreements. The new regime came into place under amendment of the federal Mines and Mineral Act and enactment of the provincial Oils Sands Royalty Regulation 1997. Some final details were different than task force recommendations, but the fact is, it worked.

The most important item was a new one percent gross provincial royalty until payout, defined as when the developer has recovered costs plus a moderate return equal to the Government of Canada bond rate. The formula is based on project revenues and costs, subject to government audit. After payout, the royalty is the greater of either one percent of gross revenues or 25 percent of net revenues. The one percent rate before payout was designed to rule out direct government participation through grants, loans, loan guarantees or other deals. The federal government increased credits on capital costs.

Newell recalls other aspects of the task force that made it a winning proposition. It created a general understanding of the great prize to be won in the oil sands for investors, oil companies, governments and Alberta's people. Pipelines were built with tie-in capabilities. All the pieces were starting to fall together.

Then came the rush.

Besides ongoing Suncor and Syncrude expansions, here's a quick look at others. The list is by no means complete.

Horizon

Canadian Natural Resources Ltd. (CNRL) of Calgary expects the $10.8-billion open-pit Horizon Oil Sands Project to begin producing 10,000 barrels per day in 2008. Construction began in 2005, about 70 kilometres north of Fort McMurray beside the Athabasca River, and will continue through 2008, when total production is planned to reach 232,000 barrels per day of synthetic crude oil.

CNRL estimates that Horizon will spin off $24 billion to Alberta and Canada over the project's 40-year lifespan. It will employ about 6000 people at peak construction. At full capacity in 2012, Horizon is expected to employ 2400 workers.

In 1989, CNRL was a struggling oil and natural gas company operating only in Alberta with nine staff, producing about 1400 barrels of oil equivalent per day. Calgary investor Murray Edwards bought in and began rebuilding. CNRL now has operations in North America, West Africa and the North Sea.

Long Lake

A joint venture between Nexen Petroleum Canada and OPTI Canada Inc. located 40 kilometres southeast of Fort McMurray, the Long Lake project boasts proprietary technology that is expected to reduce per-barrel operating costs to a comparatively low $5 to $9 per barrel. Long Lake sits on deep deposits, so it will employ SAGD for in-situ recovery. Recovered bitumen will be fed into an on-site energy-efficient upgrader, where residue will be converted into fuel gas to run operations. Phase One, estimated at $3.84 billion, will produce 70,000 barrels per day from 81 SAGD well pairs. Phase Two is estimated

at $2.79 billion and will produce another 70,000 barrels
per day.

Jackpine

Shell Canada and its partners Chevron Canada and
Western Oil Sands L.P. won regulatory approval for the
$2 billion Jackpine project in 2004, but said it would have
to wait until the expansion at its Athabasca Oil Sands Project (AOSP) was finished. The two main AOSP elements
are the Muskeg River mine, 75 kilometres north of Fort
McMurray, and the Scotford upgrader, northeast of
Edmonton. Jackpine might not go until 2010, but once in
operation, it will produce 200,000 barrels per day and will
include a mine, extraction plant, co-generation plant and
closed-loop water pipeline.

Fort Hills

Petro-Canada, UTS Energy Corp. and Teck Cominco
said in August 2006 that the Fort Hills project, about
90 kilometres north of Fort McMurray, may double in cost
from original estimates of about $5 billion to $10.5 billion.
A second stage could increase the total to $15 billion. Petro-
Canada, 55 percent shareholder and operator, said Fort
Hills spending would soar because of an increase in the
project size, plus higher labour and material costs. Instead
of the first-planned 100,000-barrels-per-day production,
Fort Hills is now planning 170,000 barrels per day.

Northern Lights

The Northern Lights mine site is about 100 kilometres
north of Fort McMurray, but the project includes an
upgrader closer to Edmonton. Operator Synenco Energy
Inc. partnered with SinoCanada Petroleum Corporation,
the Canadian subsidiary of China-based Sinopec International Petroleum Exploration and Production Corporation,

to complete the $5.3-billion, 100,000-barrel-per-day project in two phases, the final in place by 2012.

Surmont

Syncrude shareholder ConocoPhillips Canada wants to use Athabasca oil sands bitumen as feedstock for its U.S. parents' refineries. Production at the SAGD operation southeast of Fort McMurray is expected to reach 100,000 barrels per day by 2012. Surmont is estimated to cost $2.8 billion.

Tucker Lake and Sunrise

Husky Energy plans to tie its first oil sands project, Tucker Lake, about 30 kilometres northwest of Cold Lake, into its existing pipeline and upgrading facilities. Tucker, a 35,000-barrel-a-day SAGD initiative, was completed in 2006 at a cost of $500 million.

Sunrise, Husky's second oil sands venture, located 60 kilometres northeast of Fort McMurray, is estimated at $2.7 billion. It will initially produce 50,000 barrels a day but could be increased to 200,000 a day.

Kearl Lake

A partnership between Imperial Oil and ExxonMobil, the Kearl Lake oil sands project, located 70 kilometres north of Fort McMurray, will initially produce 100,000 barrels a day but will be increased eventually to 300,000 a day. Total project cost could be as much as $6.5 billion.

Christina Lake

About 120 kilometres south of Fort McMurray, Christina Lake is EnCana's largest oil sands play. Starting at about $400-million for 6000 barrels per day in 2006, Christina Lake could eventually grow to 250,000 barrels per day.

ALBERTA'S OIL PATCH

Hangingstone

Japan Canada Oil Sands Ltd. operates a 10,000-barrel-per-day pilot project at Hangingstone, but has proposed a $450-million expansion, perhaps beginning in 2008.

Sturgeon County

Sitting immediately north of Edmonton, Sturgeon County, for most of its history, was an agricultural community. That all changed with the oil sands blitz. By the middle of 2006, Sturgeon County was the proposed site for three upgraders connected to Athabasca oil sands projects (Fort Hills, Northern Lights and independent North West Upgrading Inc.), plus a biodiesel plant. Suddenly, the county found itself transforming from a rural to an industrial base.

Eric Newell, who retired from Syncrude in 2003, shakes his head in amazement at the extent of Athabasca oil sands development, but with a sense of pride.

"If you ever look at the Syncrude vision statement, we talk about the heart to win the race," said Newell. "Securing Canada's energy future. The race we're referring to there is between the oil sands of Canada and Venezuela. Back in the mid-1990s, Venezuela had all these big oil projects on. Remember, the parity point is Chicago. You're fighting for the big market. We couldn't just sit back. We were in a race against Venezuela, and they would be pushing up from the Gulf Coast. We were pushing down from Alberta.

"We won that race."

Bitumania

In early summer 2006, former premier and Alberta defender Peter Lougheed surprised many people when he raised concerns about the oil sands blitz and even called for a moratorium on new projects. He argued that using clean-burning natural gas for oil sands development was wrong when it could be used instead to develop a longer-lasting petrochemical industry. And Lougheed expressed concern that the mad rush in the oil sands was overwhelming the region's infrastructure. The former premier's argument garnered a shrug from sitting Premier Ralph Klein, but it certainly carried influence. His comments fuelled the debate over the province's financial and social returns from oil sands development.

CHAPTER TWENTY-SIX

Wiebo Ludwig
A Religious Firebrand Takes on Big Oil

GREY-HAIRED AND BEARDED LIKE A BIBLICAL PROPHET, WIEBO LUDWIG became the poster boy for opposition to oil development in Alberta. And 16-year-old Karman Willis was its innocent victim.

In 1998, at the peak of a series of vandalism and bombings of oil installations to protest development, Ludwig was charged in one incident but remained defiant in an interview with the *Edmonton Sun*. "It'll get worse before it gets better," Ludwig warned. "People are fed up. There's lots of quiet anger out there—and that's dangerous."

He was right. It was dangerous, and it did get worse.

Born in Holland, Ludwig immigrated with his family in 1952 to Rocky Mountain House and grew up in central Alberta, selling vegetables door to door to help his struggling family. He studied divinity in the U.S., and by the time he was 39, he had become the leader of the Christian Reformed Church in Goderich, Ontario. The preacher took a hard line. Ludwig berated church members for unclean living, marrying outside the church or sending children to non-Christian schools. Anyone who disagreed was placed under censure and denied communion. Some parishioners rebelled against his harsh interpretation of Christian doctrine, which included scolding working women because they weren't home with their children.

Ludwig, along with a small group of followers, established a new church that they called Our Shepherd King. They set out looking for their paradise and trekked across North America before settling in the Peace River region in 1985.

Northwest of Grande Prairie, near the BC border, about 12 kilometres southeast of Hythe, Ludwig and his entourage set up on 65 hectares that they named Trickle Creek. In addition to Ludwig's clan, Trickle Creek was also home to the Boonstra family. Richard Boonstra was also a Dutch immigrant. He'd met Ludwig in Goderich and liked the no-nonsense spiritual approach to life. In all, the two families included 15 people. The children were educated at home, men were expected to care for their women and children and the weak and to provide a living, while women tended children and raised food. The group made it clear they wanted to be left to their own ways.

Trouble began in 1990 when a Ranchmen's Resources Ltd. landman called Trickle Creek to discuss terms for survey and gas well development on the farmland. Ludwig brushed him off; the fiery reverend wasn't about to let the oil industry interrupt the small piece of heaven Our Shepherd King was slowly creating. But Ranchmen's persisted. Eventually, the company simply dispatched surveyors to the farm. Ludwig met them at the gate carrying a .30-.30 rifle.

It would be wrong to say that was the beginning of the war between the energy industry and landowners. There had been complaints and conflict all across Alberta by property owners, particularly farmers, who felt that the province's legislation gave far too much power to oil companies. There is a litany of objection about spills and leaks that people connect to illness and death in both livestock and humans. But the day Ranchmen's met a rifle-toting

Ludwig marks the beginning of one of the most damaging chapters in the ongoing conflict.

The Ranchmen's landman then obtained a court order allowing the survey to proceed. When he drove out to Trickle Creek to serve the order, Ludwig tossed the papers back into the man's car and threw him off the property. Ludwig also appealed to the Energy Resources and Conservation Board (ERCB). It didn't do any good. A drilling crew appeared in the summer and set up just south of the Ludwig fence line—the battle lines were being drawn.

In September 1990, the ERCB held a hearing on the Ludwig complaint but gave the nod to the Ranchmen's well, pending a second hearing once production began. On January 13, 1991, a separator gauge burst, releasing 59 cubic metres of raw gas. The leak was quickly contained and repaired, but Ludwig was less than impressed with Alberta's regulatory control.

That spring, Ludwig's wife Mamie Lou miscarried, her first loss after 11 healthy pregnancies. In addition, Harmony, Trickle Creek's shepherdess, counted 20 stillborn lambs among 55 born that spring. Goats also aborted. There had previously been no problems with stillborns among the livestock.

In 1993, after at least two other energy companies began operations around Trickle Creek, an unsettled Ludwig demanded the ERCB provide the second hearing, as promised. During the October hearing in Grande Prairie, Ludwig was asked if the Trickle Creek family could co-exist with the gas development. "I can co-exist with a Nazi camp supervisor if I am a captive," he answered. Ludwig complained that there was no guarantee of safety from the gas well.

In the end, the ERCB gave operational approval, calling for dialogue, planning and regulation.

On December 12, the well site supervisor ignored orders and vented 1694 cubic metres of raw gas containing more than three percent hydrogen sulphide (H_2S). The leak caused vomiting and headaches at Trickle Creek, and Ludwig put in an angry complaint to the ERCB.

By 1996, Alberta Energy Company (AEC) had bought out most of the mineral rights in the area. Norcen and Suncor were also operating in the region, and the number of wells in the area, along with flaring, increased dramatically.

Soon reports starting coming in from oil crews about an unusually high number of flat tires. There were also incidents in which Trickle Creek members accosted energy workers. Tension began to build, media took notice, and Wiebo Ludwig was good for a quote. The Ludwigs were establishing a reputation in the area as troublemakers, but they weren't without support. Plenty of people had been treated badly by Big Oil.

Vandalism at oil sites was on the rise. Cables were cut, shots were fired into shacks and tanks, acid was poured over valves and other parts were broken. In early 1997, Ludwig's son Ben was captured on security video vandalizing a hut at the former Ranchmen's wellsite. That was followed by a bizarre incident on January 2, 1997, in which Ludwig popped up at the AEC office in Grande Prairie, pulled a bottle from his pocket and dumped sour crude around the office. He did the same thing a few minutes later at the offices of the Energy and Utilities Board (formerly the ERCB). The RCMP charged both Ludwig and his son Ben. Ludwig later received a conditional discharge, with the judge suggesting that he deserved a "more widespread forum" to discuss his views. Ben got three years' probation and was ordered to pay $890 in damages.

The Ludwigs produced a home video describing their plight, entitled *Home Sour Home*. It would become a regular weapon in their public relations arsenal.

As the war of words continued to build, the AEC delivered a $300,000 statement of claim against all the Ludwigs, even including his seven-year-old son. In the spring of 1997, AEC spent $500,000 to repair a pipeline in which vandals had drilled holes. That same year, the AEC drastically increased output at its Hythe Brainard plant, which included significant flaring of excess gas. Neighbours complained bitterly of noise and pollution and blamed the flaring for trees dying and well water going bad. Early evening one day in October that year, a shot was fired into the plant office, and though no one was hit, staff were scared and upset. In the wake of the shooting, threatening letters arrived at the plant. Ludwig never claimed responsibility but made statements endorsing the action.

By early January 1998, the situation was so extraordinary that AEC president Gwyn Morgan agreed to meet with Ludwig in Edmonton. But the meeting didn't result in much more than talk, though the AEC did put its lawsuit on hold. And by April of that year, the AEC was in talks to buy out the Ludwigs, something the Trickle Creek group had been asking about for some time. However, when the official $800,000 offer came through, it included stipulations restricting them from the area and required secrecy about the deal and any environmental problems they had encountered. The Ludwigs debated the offer and rejected it.

"This company needs to get it through their head they can't puke on people," Ludwig told an AEC staffer assigned to deal with him.

On July 31, a bomb tore apart a pipeline near Hythe, followed by a second blast two days later, which ruptured a high-pressure sour gas pipeline near the Hythe Brainard plant. Serious levels of H_2S were measured in the air around the blast site. Mounties estimate that 2.27 kilograms of dynamite had been used in the first blast. The police also found evidence suggesting the same person or people had committed both crimes. The explosions took the entire issue to a new level. The community was fearful but also outraged.

Trickle Creek was equally enraged that summer. On August 21, Renee Ludwig, wife of Wiebo Ludwig Jr., delivered a deformed, stillborn boy. Ludwig recalled a Norcen spill in the area in January.

That was followed by a critical incident in which an RCMP surveillance team followed a van from the Trickle Creek compound into the Grande Cache area. Cops staked out a Suncor battery where they believed the group had been. The battery exploded at about 5:00 AM with the RCMP standing guard.

Wiebo Ludwig, Mamie Lou, Wiebo Jr. and Richard Boonstra were all charged in late August with mischief endangering life. "Some issues are worth going to jail for," Ludwig told police at the Grande Cache detachment. However, the Crown determined there wasn't enough evidence to support a conviction and withdrew the charges in September.

By this time, 160 acts of vandalism or violence had been recorded at oil installations across northern Alberta.

A $100,000 reward—$50,000 from the AEC and $50,000 from businessmen and concerned citizens—was available to anyone who could provide information that would lead to conviction.

In mid-September, the AEC decided to try a new strategy and held a Calgary press conference. "We are mystified and dismayed that people would resort to such violent acts," Gwyn Morgan said. "We don't know who is doing them, and we don't understand why. I call industrial terrorism a creeping sickness that must be eradicated."

It did little to impress the Ludwigs, who simply declared the oil industry their arch-enemy.

The RCMP, realizing it needed concrete evidence to end the Ludwig saga, set about plotting a fake oil well bombing. The plan was that a Ludwig acquaintance and sometime sympathizer named Robert Wraight would infiltrate Trickle Creek as an informer. The opportunity arose after Wraight had a change of heart and approached police. The plan was established with the assistance of Morgan and the AEC. The staged blast occurred on October 14. Police played up the angle about growing danger to the public. Resentment in the Hythe region grew.

At last, in January 1999, armed with evidence from a $750,000 investigation, the RCMP arrested Ludwig and Boonstra, with nine charges against each man. During their bail hearing, a defence attorney revealed the RCMP fake oil well bombing—sparking an international firestorm of media interest. Morgan responded with full-page advertisements in newspapers defending AEC's involvement.

In April, while Ludwig and Mamie Lou were in Edmonton for meetings, their van exploded in a hotel parking lot. Ludwig, who was standing nearby, got a cut to the forehead from flying debris. Police said it looked like the work of a professional. "This has to be attempted murder," said Boonstra. No one was charged. Police in 2006 said the file remains open.

When the preliminary hearing for Ludwig and Boonstra got underway in May, crown lawyers turned up at court in Grande Prairie wearing bulletproof vests.

If all of that wasn't enough, the Ludwig story was about to take its most tragic turn. On June 20, a group of teenagers in two vehicles decided to play a prank on the Ludwigs by joyriding through Trickle Creek property. The terrified residents of Trickle Creek, now wary because they had received a number of death threats, opened fire. A bullet penetrated one of the trucks, hit the arm of a 19-year-old boy and then struck 16-year-old Karman Willis, the girlfriend of the driver. Karman cried out; she was bleeding from the chest. Her friends drove her to hospital in Beaverlodge, but she died in an ambulance during the transfer to Grande Prairie. A group of Trickle Creek youngsters were sleeping in a tent on the property when the joyriders came through. "They went right by yelling, and we were pretty scared by that," Mamie Jr. told reporters later. "They were coming straight for our tent, then veered off just before."

A 12-man RCMP special weapons and tactics unit surrounded Trickle Creek. There was a tense standoff before police were able to safely move in and begin questioning.

Redheaded Karman Willis loved sports, particularly hockey, and was a stalwart on the local girls' squad. She was raised on a farm and had the sturdy character that goes with that upbringing. For example, a broken foot had to be set in a new cast six times because she insisted on riding her bicycle despite the injury.

After her death, Ludwig hardly offered condolences. Although he offered some sympathy to her family, he noted, with some public support, that the incident would not have occurred had the teens not been joyriding at Trickle Creek. Nor did Ludwig offer any solid evidence about who fired the fatal shot (nor did anyone else). He also blamed parents of the teens involved: "They have to reflect on the part they played in it. It's a travesty of human behaviour to allow a 16-year-old out at 4:00 AM doing things like this."

No charges were ever laid in Karman Willis' death.

Soon, signs began appearing at businesses in Hythe and Beaverlodge, denying service to Trickle Creek members.

The trial of Ludwig and Boonstra finally began in February 2000 with AEC staff and Wraight providing key testimony. But tapes made by Wraight were so distorted that the judge threw out the transcripts. He allowed the tapes to be played, but most were so rough they couldn't be deciphered.

A standing-room-only crowd was on hand on April 19 when Ludwig was declared guilty on five charges of oil patch vandalism. Boonstra was found guilty on one mischief charge. On April 26, Ludwig was sentenced to 28 months in prison; Boonstra got 21 days.

After his statutory release in November 2001, Ludwig pledged: "I'm more determined than ever. I'll say that. Jail hasn't slowed me down in terms of addressing these problems. It's only deepened my resolve that this needs to be dealt with."

The AEC estimated it had cost $10 million to deal with Ludwig-related issues.

The Edmonton Fringe Festival provided a postscript on the Ludwig plot. In 2002, Ludwig and other members of his clan were invited to the Fringe to watch a play about his dispute with the oil industry. Afterwards, he gave the play two thumbs up.

Bitumania

In a July 2006 edition of *Rolling Stone* magazine, former U.S. vice-president Al Gore, a potential presidential candidate, blasted oil sands developers in Alberta. "For every barrel of oil they extract there, they have to use enough natural gas to heat a family's home for four days," said Gore. "And they have to tear up four tons of landscape, all for one barrel of oil. It is truly nuts." Gore, promoting his documentary about global warming called *An Inconvenient Truth*, likened oil sands developers to junkies. His comments earned typical contempt from Premier Ralph Klein: "The United States needs our oil. I don't know what he proposes the world run on, maybe hot air?"

CHAPTER TWENTY-SEVEN

Ralph Klein
The Former Calgary Mayor Uses Resource Wealth to Build a Massive Surplus

ALBERTANS WILL LIKELY REMEMBER RALPH KLEIN AS THE PREMIER WHO doled out $400 in "prosperity cheques" to each person in the province, but for Eastern Canadians he'll always be known for the "creeps and bums" flap. He has a well-known affinity for alcohol and admits to enjoying gambling, traits that have caused him embarrassment but at the same time showed him to be a person of normal faults, endearing him further to the public.

Klein rose from modest German-immigrant roots first into media, then civic politics, then the provincial cabinet and finally into the premier's office. During his premiership from 1992 to 2006, Klein took Alberta from a $23 billion debt to an $8 billion surplus, based on a combination of severe spending cuts and giant gains in energy royalty payments thanks to high world prices, and he garnered a huge base of political popularity.

His grandfather Andrew emigrated through New York in 1906, heard about the wide-open spaces, available land and opportunity in Western Canada and came to Alberta in 1907. He had four children, including a son, the youngest, named Philip, born in 1917. Philip and his sisters grew up tough and broke and learned independence. Phil Klein worked a variety of jobs across the prairies. In the Dirty '30s, he used his schoolyard fighting skills to earn a few extra bucks in the boxing ring but later switched to professional wrestling under the ring name "Killer Klein."

Future premier Ralph Klein was born on November 1, 1942, in Calgary. He grew up with plenty of friends but showed little hint of his future success. Young Ralph didn't like sports but loved outdoor activities such as fishing. In school, Klein achieved at average or less, and he admits he never really tried. During the Joseph McCarthy political witch hunts from 1951 through 1954 in the U.S., Klein occasionally went by the name Ralph MacBeth (the sur-name of his mother's second husband) to avoid publicizing his German roots.

After school came a few jobs here and there followed by a stint in the Royal Canadian Air Force, which instilled a sense of discipline but also made him homesick. Klein then entered Calgary Business College, where he shook off his reputation for poor performance, did well in account-ing and commercial law and graduated with honours.

After a short stint in teaching, Klein moved into public relations, an arena in which he proved to be an expert. But while working with the Canadian Red Cross, Klein discovered an affinity for the reporters he worked with. He liked the style. They were a group of tight-knit smokers and drinkers who made stories by building relationships. Klein took a reporting position with CFCN Television in Calgary and was eventually assigned to cover Calgary city council through the 1970s.

In the summer of 1980, he announced his intention to run for mayor, a move that was initially taken as a joke. He was shrugged off as an also-ran, but polls showed that a significant number of Calgary voters were undecided. Klein signed on Rod Love, who would be the ongoing architect of much of his future political success, to his campaign. Love eyed the undecided vote, and together they set a course that let the two frontrunners stumble over each other, while Klein picked up the slack. Klein's $30,000 campaign left him $12,000 in debt, but he stunned the city by winning the mayoralty on October 15, 1980.

The Ralph Klein political era was underway.

Only two weeks after Klein's election in Calgary, the federal government announced the National Energy Program, which had devastating results for Alberta's economy. In 1981, Calgary's Olympic organizing committee won its bid for the 1988 Winter Games.

On January 6, 1982, the rookie mayor gave a speech to the Calgary Newcomer's Club in which, with typical Klein shoot-from-the-hip style, he criticized the "creeps" who were flowing to Calgary job hunting and promised "cowboy techniques" for those that committed crime. A *Calgary Herald* reporter broke the story the following morning under the headline "Stay Away, Bums Told." The story erupted in a gusher of retaliatory rhetoric and media hype right across the country.

The creeps and bums controversy eventually waned, but the NEP impact was still building, and the province's economy turned dismal when the world oil price collapsed. Klein maintained a spirit of optimism and his appeal to the average Calgarian, winning a second term as mayor in October 1983, and a third in 1986, the latter by the largest margin of victory in the history of Calgary.

Conservative Premier Don Getty, looking to boost the sagging popularity of his party, approached Klein in 1988 to ask him to enter provincial politics. Klein asked for a cabinet appointment, and Getty surprised him by agreeing.

When word got out, veteran Tories were outraged by the audacity of the newcomer. Klein ran in Calgary-Elbow and on March 29, 1989, won a close victory but saw his mentor, Getty, go down in defeat in Edmonton.

While Getty looked about for a safe riding to win his way back into election, Klein was assigned as the post of minister of environment, which he at first considered a step down from the Calgary mayor's chair. But Klein went about cabinet business with his typical style, extensively consulting with the public on a range of new legislation. And it didn't hurt that environment was emerging as top public concern. The newcomer also quickly began garnering support from junior members of the Tory caucus, gladly abandoning Edmonton, which he openly disliked, to take up invitations to MLA functions around the province.

Getty quit in 1992, switching Klein's leadership team into high gear. The main adversary was Edmonton's Nancy Betkowski, considered a front-runner and a favourite among women. But Klein's camp took better advantage of a new system for the leadership vote, in which the delegate process was eliminated in favour of one vote for each party member. On December 5, 1992, after an ugly campaign with some hurtful mudslinging at Klein, the little mayor from Calgary was named Alberta's new premier. He was sworn in on December 14.

Klein immediately embarked on a campaign of severe spending cuts, which surprisingly won significant public approval. The premier's post came with a huge debt inherited from the Lougheed and Getty administrations. Klein set about ridding the weight from the taxpayers' shoulders, and got a boost from improved oil prices. By February 1995, Alberta had its first balanced budget in a decade, and then began the process of tackling the long-term debt. International media began to pick up on what was happening in the oil-rich province on the Canadian prairie. Alberta's $23-billion debt in 1992 cost $1.4 billion a year in carrying dues. Klein won his first election in June 1993, repeated victory in March 1997, took his biggest landslide in March 2001 and then won again in November 2004.

During a pancake breakfast at the Calgary Stampede in 2004, Klein held a press conference in which he announced that his government would wipe out the remaining $3.7 billion debt by March 2005.

"I've been dreaming about this day for some time now," Klein told about 1500 people. Indeed, by that March, the debt was gone, and Alberta was set to post massive surpluses. By comparison, at the same time, Ontario had a total debt of $126 billion.

"Albertans themselves deserve the credit," Klein said. "They told us to stop running deficits and start paying off the debt, and that's exactly what we did."

The province's burgeoning wealth flamed the ongoing firefight with other provinces that expected a share. A 2005 poll reported that 61 percent of people in the rest of Canada thought Alberta should share its petroleum-fuelled wealth. Klein noted that when the price of oil was low, other provinces gleefully pledged that Alberta deserved it. Some academics suggested that Alberta had a duty to help out other regions.

"We're already doing more than our share—it's about $2400 per person in Alberta that we send to the rest of Canada," Klein said, noting that Alberta remits $12 billion a year to Ottawa in equalization payments.

In 2005 and into 2006, the world price of oil started moving upwards. In late 2005, Hurricane Katrina came in, wiping out drilling rigs in the gas-rich Gulf of Mexico and swamping several major U.S. refineries. Oil prices began climbing towards all-time highs, as much as US$78 per barrel by mid-2006. The vast majority of Alberta's royalty wealth comes from natural gas, but the high oil price pushed oil industry investment and profits into high gear. The province's regular land lease sales brought in billions.

It was during 2005, the province's centennial year, that Klein began talking about returning some oil wealth to Albertans—a $1.4-billion giveaway. The official announcement came in September 2005. Each Albertan would receive a $400 "prosperity" payment. The proposal had already brought yet another storm of criticism—many people thought the money could be better spent on public needs such as hospitals, schools or roads. Klein shrugged off the debate.

"If they don't want it, send it back or make a charitable donation or do something with it," Klein said. "To some people it means a lot."

The cheques, sent out to every family member of households where a tax return had been filed, didn't actually start going out until January 2006. By then, enterprising businesses were poised to take advantage. Retailer Sears Canada offered to exchange rebate cheques in return for a $440 gift card. Fairmont Hotels offered discount $400 "Thanks Ralph" packages at its five Alberta hotels (the Jasper Park Lodge took a flurry of bookings). Furniture and appliance retailer the Brick offered to double the prosperity cheque amount for every $2000 spent at its stores. As the cheques came in, retailers were pleased with the resulting rush.

"Our sales in the shopping centre were up 12 percent in January year over year," Edmonton's Kingsway Garden Mall general manager Brad Merchant told the *Edmonton Sun*. "We were on a pretty good increasing trend before that—between seven percent and eight percent had been our medium-term trend, and it jumped another four percent. We would certainly attribute that almost entirely to the prosperity cheques."

Klein had planned to hang on to the premier's post until the end of 2007. But all observers were shocked at the March 2006 party convention when Klein only managed 55 percent support in a leadership review. His time was up. The premier called a leadership convention for the fall of 2006.

On August 31, his last day in the legislature, Klein wept during a standing ovation by MLAs, then, in his usual Ralph frankness, admitted his government hadn't properly planned for the incredible economic growth across Alberta nor in provincial coffers.

"The Opposition is right in their criticism, but as I said, no one could anticipate the phenomenal growth that took place and the quickness of that growth," the outgoing premier said. "They were right about not having a plan—a plan is being developed."

Bitumania

After the Ralph Klein government introduced deregulation of Alberta's power and natural gas systems in the late 1990s, natural gas prices began to rise. To protect consumers from the price wallop during the transition to free-market selling of natural gas, the government brought in a monthly rebate package. The program, applicable in the winter months from November through March, kicked in if most regulated prices rose above

$5.50 per gigajoule. They did. For three years, through to the winter of 2005–06, the province doled out $1.1 billion in rebates. Prices were so high in October 2005 that the province extended rebates to cover that month. Then, in February 2006, Energy Minister Greg Melchin announced a three-year extension of the winter rebate program through 2009.

CHAPTER TWENTY-EIGHT

The Billionaires
Some Calgary Oilmen are Among the Wealthiest in the World

MEN SUCH AS ERIC HARVIE, FRANK MCMAHON AND MAX BELL attained millionaire status in Alberta's oil industry. Others got even richer. Each year, *Canadian Business* magazine runs a list of Canada's wealthiest people, the billionaires. The magazine's 2006 list included three Alberta entries, each with activity in the oil industry.

Fred and Ron Mannix

Brothers Fred and Ron Mannix were both nominated to the Order of Canada in 2005, an honour bestowed on people who have well served Canada's best interests. The Mannix family is known for a range of philanthropy—donating to universities, medical research, social services and culture.

The Calgary-based Mannix family guards its privacy, and for good reason. In 1972, a neighbour's daughter was taken for ransom. After her rescue, police discovered that the true target had been Fred's wife Margaret.

The Mannix family built up a wide-ranging business empire in construction, mining, energy, finance and real estate with a reach as far as Europe and Australia. The business began with Fred Stephen Mannix, who worked on railway construction across the prairies in the late 1800s and early 1900s. Reports suggest that the elder Mannix was a skilful poker player who once bluffed with a pair of twos to win an earthmover machine. Later, he widened his corporate operations into other construction and coal mining. Mannix was also known for losing a lot of money. With mounting debt, he sold controlling interest in Fred Mannix & Co. to an American firm. By 1950, Fred Charles Mannix was able to repurchase the company, and then went on to build Mannix Co. Ltd. into a multinational. Fred Charles went to work as a teenager at his father's construction company, but first distinguished himself by drinking whiskey, playing poker, getting his nose broken in fist fights and crashing the cars that his father gave him. He capitalized on post-war reconstruction of public infrastructure such as the Trans-Canada Highway, the St. Lawrence Seaway, the Toronto subway, the Pembina pipeline and even Great Canadian Oil Sands. The firm was renamed Loram International Ltd., standing for Long Range Mannix. The family simply called its business "the outfit."

Famed Alberta Premier Peter Lougheed was a Loram vice-president. At one point, the Mannix conglomerate held more than 130 firms. The senior Mannix passed on corporate control to his sons Fred and Ron. *Canadian Business* estimates their wealth at $2.15 billion, ranking them, in 2005, as 13th among Canada's richest people.

Clay Riddell

High energy prices sent Calgary-based Clay Riddell soaring up the *Canadian Business* rich list in 2005. Riddell, chairman and CEO of Paramount Resources Ltd., stood 11th among Canada's wealthiest people, with an estimated fortune of $2.35 billion.

The son of a Winnipeg mailman, Riddell took a geology degree at the University of Manitoba before beginning a career in 1959 in Alberta at Chevron Corporation. Riddell scoured Alberta and the Northwest Territories for oil and gas until 1974, when he set up Paramount Oil & Gas Ltd. In 1978, Riddell issued an initial public offering for 40 percent of Paramount Resources Ltd. The offering raised $5 million capital. Twenty-five years later in 2004, Paramount Resources reported $41.4 million profit on $550.6 million sales with total assets of $1.5 billion.

"We have a lot of very patient shareholders, and they've been rewarded as a result," Riddell told *Canadian Business*. "We built our entire company by drilling and developing gas beyond the edge of the pipelines where there wasn't as much competition." It's a risky strategy going out where no one else is working. It can take years to bring in production and even longer to make a profit.

In an interview with Diane Francis of the *National Post*, Riddell recalled Paramount's beginnings, when he wanted to avoid takeover and outside influence from investment houses. "I wanted to control my own destiny," Riddell said. "We didn't have any production until 1981. I remember at an annual meeting one of my investors handed me a note scratched on a brown bag that said I had come across the formula for going bankrupt: no gas, loans up, losses up. But in this business, you must have the ability to be patient, and to be patient, you can't be without control."

He told *Oilweek* that he drilled nine dry holes in a row. "The 10th and final well I only drilled because I was stubborn. The investors were getting nervous. It didn't look much better, but I ran production casing and managed to test a little gas."

Riddell's patience and persistence was also matched by skills in his trade. He led the development of a technique to use compressed air to control well pressure. Eventually, with enough producing wells, Riddell was able to convince pipeline operators to move into his most productive areas and hook him up. Either that or he built his own pipeline.

Along the way, Paramount survived the devastating National Energy Program, which chased away investment. Then in 2001 and 2002, Paramount got into a battle with Alberta regulators. Heavy oil producers in the Athabasca oil sands region complained that gas extraction was destabilizing the geology and threatening their output. The province forced gas producers in the area, Paramount being the largest of the group, to shut down their wells.

"I honestly thought we were done with it then," Riddell told *Oilweek*. "I was so angry and possessed by the injustice of the whole thing. It really destroyed our engines of growth."

In 2002, Paramount spun out Paramount Energy Trust, now headed up by Riddell's daughter Susan Riddell Rose. Son Jim Riddell is president and chief operating officers of Paramount Resources.

Murray Edwards

Murray Edwards had managed to save about $100,000 by the time he was 28. He turned that into billions by investing in hard-pressed companies and turning them around. One of those was Canadian Natural Resources Limited (CNRL), which is now a major oil sands project owner and operator.

Born and raised in Regina, Edwards took a commerce degree at the University of Saskatchewan and then completed a law degree at the University of Toronto, before embarking on a stint at a Calgary law firm. Edwards decided to change his life after a close friend died of a brain tumour at age 27. "I began thinking that maybe I should go out and make a go of it. That experience taught me life is fleeting. You have to chase your dreams."

Edwards used his savings from his time in law practice to join some partners who bought into CNRL, which was a far cry from the juggernaut it is today. At that time, CNRL was a tiny firm on the verge of bankruptcy and selling at pennies a share. Edwards and his partners set about acquiring other energy firms and discovering new oil and gas deposits. They took CNRL revenue to $18 million in two years, with a 6000 percent gain on stock value.

"I'm basically a contrarian investor," he told *Canadian Business*. "I buy at the bottom of the business cycle, when companies are cheap. There is no secret to my success. It's all just hard work."

With success under his belt, Edwards began investing in other companies. He's invested in aerospace, metals, mining and resorts. Wherever he turns his interest, he's been able to take floundering companies and turn them around. Edwards is noted for skill and timing in buying assets that seem out of favour. He's been called the Wayne Gretzky of the oil patch.

Edwards is president and owner of Edco Financial Holdings Ltd. based in Calgary. He owns Resorts of the Canadian Rockies and is a principal of Penn West Energy Trust, Magellan Aerospace Corp. and Ensign Resource Service Group.

CNRL is now in the early stages of its flagship Horizon Oil Sands Project in northeastern Alberta. Horizon is expected to cost $10 billion to set up. At full production in 2012, Horizon will produce 232,000 barrels of oil per day.

"Who would have thought that in January 1989, when CRNL was worth about $20 million and our vice-chairman Murray Edwards rescued us from the bank?" said co-chairman Allan Markin at a September 2005 opening of the Horizon oil sands aerodrome. "We got in the oil and gas business in the United States and didn't do too well. Today, we're doing a $10-billion project, and the asset value of our company is about $30 billion. That's a long way in 16 years—$20 million to $30 billion."

CNRL continues its growth pattern. In September 2006, the Calgary oil company announced a $4.075 billion U.S. takeover of Anadarko Petroleum Corp.'s western Canadian natural gas assets.

Bitumania

In January 2006, the popular long-running U.S. news program *60 Minutes* featured a Sunday night story on Alberta's oil sands, focusing on the growing importance of the resource for North America markets. When stock markets opened Monday, share prices of Canadian energy companies shot up, some setting record highs. "Two words: *60 Minutes*," is how one analyst explained the gains to reporters. Suncor's stock had gained three percent by the closing bell and reached a record high of $87.40 per share during the day before settling back a bit to $86.23. The TV program also mentioned the high wages being paid to oil sands workers. As a result, some companies reported that they received phone calls from Americans looking for work.

CHAPTER TWENTY-NINE

More Oil Politics
Kyoto Protocol, Income Trusts and Value-added Production

OIL COMES WITH A PRICE, AND NOT JUST WHAT MOTORISTS PAY AT the pump. The economics of oil changes as the resource is depleted, and the hunt goes on for new sources. Questions are asked about how Alberta should best take advantage of its energy heritage. And, of course, there is a range of issues on environmental damage.

The Kyoto Protocol

TrueNorth Energy threw up a red flag in January 2003 when it shelved its $3.3-billion Fort Hills oil sands project, citing soaring costs coupled with uncertainty over an international environmental deal.

Known generally as the Kyoto Protocol, because 160 countries negotiated a tentative agreement in that Japanese city in 1997, the deal basically called for a six percent cut in 1990 greenhouse gas (GHG) emission levels by 2012. Costs were ballooning for everyone in the oil sands, and the last thing anyone in the oil and gas business needed was more uncertainty. Echoing the National Energy Program of the early 1980s, the federal Jean Chrétien Liberal government was determined to implement Kyoto. But the protocol had problems from the outset. The deal went easy on developing nations such as China and India. And the Americans complained, for a series of reasons, that it wouldn't work and would damage their economy, so they pulled out.

Pressure was building on the Chrétien government to ratify Kyoto. In the oil industry, owners and shareholders worried. Reports suggested that the costs of implementing the emissions-reductions strategies could add up to as much as $7 per barrel. In many cases, that rendered projects such as Fort Hills unprofitable.

TrueNorth, majority owned by U.S. energy giant Koch Industries, wasn't the only one to pull the plug or delay activity in the oil sands. Despite the pride expressed by operators about their environmental standards, the grim fact remains that oil sands production, by its nature, is a dirty business. Meeting the Kyoto standards was a financial question mark that many weren't willing to risk. Some oil sands developers began talking about moving portions of their projects, such as upgraders, to U.S. locations. Calgary-based Nexen delayed its oil sands plans and went looking elsewhere in the world for development.

Eventually, Chrétien began to look for ways to implement Kyoto but still maintain oil industry support. In 2003, he pledged that Canadian ratification would not kill jobs and that the federal policy would offer research and development incentives. In a letter responding to concerns listed by the Canadian Association of Petroleum Producers, Chrétien said: "The government's intention is that future emissions-reduction targets will not make Canadian oil and gas production uncompetitive." By February 2005, the Liberal government had ratified Kyoto with no plan for implementation.

Royalty incentives already in place were enough to keep the oil sands expansion going at a wild pace. TrueNorth minority partner UTS Energy bought out Koch, and then brought in Petro-Canada and Teck Cominco as partners at Fort Hills, and the project moved ahead.

The Liberal government, beleaguered by the federal sponsorship scandal, fell to the Stephen Harper Tories in 2006. Harper ran his election campaign with a promise that Canada would opt out of Kyoto in favour of an undefined "made-in-Canada" solution. Rookie Environment Minister Rona Ambrose, an Edmonton-area MP, declared that the Kyoto targets were unattainable.

"It is impossible—impossible for Canada to reach its Kyoto target," Ambrose told media. "The next step is to start to talk about action and solutions long term. We need solutions that are out by 50, 100 years—not two years, five years."

In late May 2006, Canada agreed to take part in international negotiations for a second phase of the Kyoto Protocol. However, by October that year, the Tories' minority government under Harper introduced its Clean Air Act, which avoided use of the term Kyoto. Instead, it set a broader horizon, such as 2050 for greenhouse gas reductions, the latest of the program's goals. The program was developed under negotiations with corporate Canada, including Alberta's upstream producers, oil sands operators among them.

Income Trusts

Income trusts are publicly traded firms, but instead of offering common shares with a dividend, they sell units with distributions from cash flow. The difference is substantial, both in terms of how much money is returned to the unitholder and in how the money is taxed. A common-share company pays its businesses taxes, then sets aside some profits to be sent out to shareholders as dividends. Those shareholders then pay tax on the dividends—essentially, it is argued, paying tax twice, once as a corporation owner and again as the recipient of dividends. Income trusts, on the other hand, dole out almost all cash flow to the unitholders, who pay tax on the distribution, effectively eliminating one level of dues. The trust form became popular in the late-1990s and in the early years after the turn of the 21st century. Many Alberta energy companies with revenue-producing wells opted for the tax-favourable trust model. New firms set up as trusts, while existing players made the conversion from common-share form to trust.

Because so many companies went the income trust route, the federal government was forced in 2005 to deal with how trust unit distributions were taxed compared to common shares. It became a bit of a debacle in November that year, when a pending announcement by Finance Minister Ralph Goodale was leaked. The information sparked a streak of alleged insider trading prior to the official announcement, and the RCMP was called in to investigate. Among the income trusts that traded heavily in the questionable period were Calgary-based oil and gas trusts.

Federal officials weren't the only ones grappling with the issue. In its 2006 budget, the Alberta government offered a warning: the switch to income trusts was costing the province a net revenue loss of about $400 million per year. "Rather than paying tax at the business level, investors pay personal income tax on the income in their province of residence," the budget documents explained. "Alberta has 10 percent of Canada's population, yet over 60 percent of Canada's market capitalization for income trusts." Oil and gas firms account for the vast majority of those Alberta-based income trusts. "The shift from corporate income tax, which is taxed in Alberta, to personal income tax, which is taxed in the jurisdiction where the investor lives, means that Alberta has lost revenue and will continue to do so."

Goodale brought in adjustments to common share taxation that reduced the advantage to income trusts. Alberta soon followed suit. In September 2006, the province mimicked the feds by raising its dividend tax credit, making those investments more lucrative.

A dramatic change developed on Halloween 2006, when federal Finance Minister Jim Flaherty, in the fledging and minority Stephen Harper Tory government, waited until markets closed before announcing tax amendments that wiped out the income trust advantage. The new rules put a 31.5 percent tax on trust distributions. Income trusts on the Toronto Stock Exchange lost $20 billion in value the following day. Outrage stalked through Calgary, where so many oil and gas income trusts were based.

"I think it's excessive overkill," Bill Andrew, CEO of Penn West Energy told the *Calgary Sun*. In a quarterly conference call with analysts later that month, an American investor queried Andrew on how the oil income trusts would now proceed on the issue.

"You saw what happened at Boston Harbor?" Andrew quipped, referring to the 1773 Boston Tea Party, in which American colonists revolted against British government control.

Value-Added Production

When Hurricane Katrina blasted the Gulf of Mexico and New Orleans in late 2005, oil and gasoline prices soared in its wake. As refining and production capacity in the Gulf was shut down, it cut North American supplies, and observers took note of the need that Alberta could fill. Yet, there has been a consistent complaint that the province should be more than a provider of raw oil.

Alberta has always been a place where an oilman could take a risk, work hard to make a good living and perhaps even get rich. Oil companies provide high-paying jobs and good returns to investors. Government coffers are swollen with royalties and taxes. Yes, the energy industry has been good to the Wild Rose province. Yet oilmen and politicians know that Alberta is selling itself short by simply extracting raw resources and providing limited upgrading. The potential for greater returns—vastly greater returns—is stuck there in the muck around Athabasca, Peace River and Cold Lake.

In 2003, the province and some members of the industry formed an ad hoc group with the purpose of investigating the challenges and opportunities associated with the expansion of Alberta's petroleum products industry. The Hydrocarbon Upgrading Task Force spawned a couple of reports—one suggesting that there is huge potential for Alberta's oil patch to evolve into an industry of numerous high-value products to be sold competitively into multiple markets. The task force went about developing its vision for Alberta's oil and gas industry for the year 2020. Indeed, the future could be better.

"Alberta is Canada's largest petrochemical producing province, accounting for over $9 billion worth of products and more than $5 billion worth of exports each year," Premier Ralph Klein said in a Fort Saskatchewan speech in late 2005. "These are big numbers, and I'd like to see them get even bigger. Right now, most bitumen in Alberta is upgraded into synthetic crude oil. That's acceptable, but not ideal, to the refineries that buy it. Some crude bitumen also goes to market at a reduced price. Obviously, it would be better for Alberta to market a value-added product instead of raw bitumen or minimally upgraded synthetic crude. Ideally, I'd like to see an integrated upgrading, refining and petrochemical industry, based on bitumen from Alberta's oil sands.

"This would add tens of billions of dollars to the value of Alberta's resources and create thousands of new, high-paying jobs. There is an existing industrial infrastructure with upgraders, refineries and petrochemical plants that can be a base for further integration."

Soheil Asgarpour, a business unit leader with Alberta Energy and one of the proponents on the task force, told *Alberta Oil* magazine about the opportunity available, since many consumer products have a petroleum base.

"Most things we touch—most things we deal with—are made from petroleum products. So, the vision is when you get up in the morning in 2020, much of what you touch is going to be made from our bitumen: from the finish on your hardwood floor to the carpet that you step on, your toothbrush, the mouse you have right now on your computer. All of these things are derived from that bitumen."

Some experts suggest that the return to Albertans, in terms of jobs, profits or taxes, through a high-value petroleum-products industry cluster, could be five times to more than 20 times what it is today.

The question is, how do we get there? Greg Melchin, Alberta's Energy Minister in 2006, hopes the task force will result in an integration strategy in which government provides research assistance plus a regulatory or legal framework, enabling industry to take the reins and make the required investment. In addition, he hopes the work of the task force will be ongoing.

"There is a huge, lengthy list of products that come out of the petrochemical industry," said Melchin. "We only do a small fraction of those here in Alberta. What I hope is that we start to move into other products. First, we need a longer-term oil and gas supply to support existing industry. From there, you could have a broadened base of production here in Alberta."

Justin Riemer of Alberta Economic Development, one of the people working with the task force, said successful implementation of the vision would result in significant investment downstream—new refineries, new crackers, derivatives plants.

"Given the events of the hurricanes in the Gulf Coast and rising gasoline prices, the need for more refining capacity in North America is clear—the question is, why not in Alberta?" said Riemer. "What we're trying to be is the catalyst to get this going. No one player can do this alone. It's going to take a variety of players."

The 2020 vision sees Alberta importing raw resources from BC and Saskatchewan and from northern pipelines such as the massive proposed Alaska and Mackenzie lines. Alberta's supply in 2020 could reach three million barrels per day of bitumen, 430,000 barrels per day of oil and 283 million cubic metres per day of natural gas. The report suggests a $16-billion annual increase in Alberta shipments, two new upgrader-refineries, two new flexi-feed crackers, eight new derivative plants and 30 other manufacturing facilities. Investment is estimated at $100 billion.

But of course, at this point anyway, it's all just a pipe dream.

Coalbed Methane

Another area of potential energy gain comes from coalbed methane (CBM). It's the natural gas hidden in coal formations, absorbed onto the surface of the coal. Generally, the higher grade the coal, the more methane it has absorbed. Coal can store up to seven times more gas than a typical gas reservoir. But it's tough to get at, requiring more wells over the area. The Energy and Utilities Board expects CBM production in the province to reach 15.26 billion cubic metres by 2014. That would be about 12 percent of the province's total gas production, up from less than one percent in 2004.

The most promising CBM opportunity is the Mannville coal zone, a vast sweep from the BC border near Grande Prairie east to Lloydminster. But farmers and ranchers are worried. CBM development in the U.S. has a poor record, causing land and water damage.

Bitumania

Oil sands development in Athabasca came to royal attention in May 2005, when Prince Philip, the Duke of Edinburgh, toured operations. Arriving at Suncor's Steepbank mine in a military helicopter accompanied by oil sands officials in two other choppers, the prince climbed aboard a Caterpillar 797, one of the iconic sand-hauling dump trucks, as big as a typical house and with wheels twice as tall as a man. In the cab of the truck, he met driver Tracey Gladue, a 29-year-old mother of one. "It was awesome," Gladue told *Fort McMurray Today*. "He was very personable, and he set the tone right away. It was very comfortable talking to him. It was an excellent experience. He was very involved in the facts and technology of the truck. It was a once in a lifetime opportunity. I don't think something like this will happen again. But I could live without all of the media attention."

CHAPTER THIRTY

The Spy Game
Scouts Trade Information—A Commodity More Valuable than Oil

ALBERTA'S OIL INDUSTRY HAS ITS SECRETS, AND THERE ARE WELL-PAID sleuths trying to uncover them. Known as "scouts," Alberta's oil patch spies arm themselves with four-by-fours, ATVs, binoculars, survival kits, sensors and anything else they need to head out on to the barren prairie or into the thick bush to stake out rigs and other operations.

In 1998, one such scout boasted to an Edmonton newspaper that he was making the well-above-average salary of $100,000 a year—though he considered it more like danger pay. He recounted an incident in which he hid in the bush along the BC-Alberta border and, using a high-powered scope, counted lengths of pipe pulled out of a drill hole to estimate its depth. He then hid his ATV nearby and set off in his truck to get some rest. When he returned, the ATV's starter had been cut away—a warning that he'd been discovered.

Scouts have also been known to drink with off-duty rig workers, buying rounds in a bid to loosen tongues with booze. At one time, a group of scouts held weekly information-exchange meetings at a Calgary hotel. They've also been known to use illegal tactics such as intercepting phone calls or faxes and will even sneak right into a rig shack to take a peak at the logbook. Drilling crews know the scouts are watching, and there have been fights. Workers have even dumped motor oil on rig floors to fool scouts into thinking there had been a strike.

Oil companies use scout information to protect their investments—or avoid making them. Former Canadian 88 President Greg Noval told the *Edmonton Sun* that oil scout information prevented his company from making a $400-million investment mistake. A potential takeover target said it had a major discovery, but details gleaned by a scout showed the strike wasn't as big as suggested. Noval even said Canadian 88 hired scouts to keep tabs on the company's own people—in case some were spies selling information to competitors. "The idea is to do the scouting, not be scouted," Noval told the *Edmonton Sun.* "It's one of the tools of a very high-risk, high-reward business."

One of the earliest recorded scouts was George "Jonesy" Jones, who worked for Royalite Oil Co. in the Turner Valley field. According to *In the Light of the Flares: History of Turner Valley Oil Fields,* some of Jonesy's discoveries led to important acquisitions.

The story of spying in the Alberta oil patch took a much more sinister turn in the wake of the 2001 terrorist strikes in the U.S. In 2002, ATCO boss Nancy Southern confirmed reported that foreign spies had inspected one of her company's natural gas processing plants just two months before the 9/11 New York and Washington, DC, terrorist attacks of 2001. "I can tell you that we are aware of agents of foreign powers that have been touring our facilities," Southern told a counterterrorism conference in Calgary. "And I can tell you, as a result, we have increased our threat assessments and our security, and conducted significantly more security audits in all of our facilities."

ATCO undertook a thorough security review after the U.S. terrorist strikes and learned from staff of the suspicious pair that had visited the gas plant. ATCO reported the incident, and in turn, Alberta's solicitor general's department notified the Canadian Security Intelligence Service. A provincial spokesman said the suspects were "well-known agents of a foreign power who are capable of posing a threat to Canada."

Southern bemoaned the new world order. "Security in the past has been dedicated to theft, fraud, corporate espionage," Southern told reporters. "We have never, as corporates, been exposed to the threat of crippling critical services to undermine the strength of a community—and that's the paradigm shift the corporates are having to face today."

In early June 2006, police in Toronto swept down on an alleged terrorist cell and arrested 17 people, some of them youths. The bust came as a shocking wake-up call for Canadians, since terrorism was usually thought to be something that other countries had to worry about. This was the first indication of wider terrorist activity within their own border, and they shuddered.

In the wake of the arrests, experts pointed to Alberta's abundant energy infrastructure as an obvious terrorist target. But the EUB said it had been working on security issues since the 9/11 strikes, and requires energy providers that operate "critical" infrastructure to have in place "terrorism mitigation strategies." Those strategies are periodically reviewed and updated. In addition, the board does spot security audits.

It is another indication of how much Alberta's energy industry has changed since Wa Pa Su arrived in 1719 at

York Factory on Hudson's Bay carrying a small sample of
sticky bitumen.

Notes on Sources

Alberta in the 20th Century, Volume 1: The Great West Before 1900. Edmonton: United Western Communications, 1991.

Alberta in the 20th Century, Volume 3: The Boom and the Bust 1910–1914. Edmonton: United Western Communications, 1994.

Alberta in the 20th Century, Volume 7: Aberhart and the Albertan Insurrection 1935–1940. Edmonton: United Western Communications, 1998.

Alberta in the 20th Century, Volume 9: Leduc, Manning and the Age of Prosperity. Edmonton: United Western Communications, 2001

Alberta in the 20th Century, Volume 11: Lougheed & the War with Ottawa 1971–1984. Edmonton: History Book Publications, 2003.

Alberta in the 20th Century, Volume 12: Alberta Takes the Lead 1984–2000. Edmonton: History Book Publications, 2003.

Annual Report, Indian Oil and Gas Canada, 2005–2006.

"Atco Boosts Security in Wake of Tour by Spies." *Edmonton Sun*, November 8, 2002, 73.

Blake, Melissa, Mayor, Wood Buffalo Regional Municipality. Interview, September 25, 2006.

Blegen, Theodore C. *Five Fur Traders of the Northwest*. St. Paul: Minnesota Historical Society, 1965.

Bolton, Ken, Sharon A.Fogarty, Donaleen Saul, and Sheonaid Ursan. *The Albertans*. Edmonton: Lone Pine Publishing, 1981.

Breen, David H. *Alberta's Petroleum Industry and the Conservation Board*. Edmonton: University of Alberta Press, 1993.

Bradley, Kim. "Ludwig Van Blasted." *Edmonton Sun*, April 20, 1999, 3.

Brennan, Brian. "Vern 'Dryhole' Hunter." *Alberta Oil, the Magazine*, Volume 1, Issue 3, 2005, 62–63.

Brennan, Brian. *Building a Province: 60 Alberta Lives*. Calgary: Fifth House, 2000.

Brennan, Brian. *Alberta Originals: Stories of Albertans Who Made a Difference*. Calgary: Fifth House, 2001.

Budget 2006, Province of Alberta.

Bussieres, Lance. Interview, May 25, 2006.

"Canada's Oil Sands, a Supply and Market Outlook to 2015." National Energy Board, October 2000.

Chastko, Paul. *Developing Alberta's Oil Sands: From Karl Clark to Kyoto*. Calgary: University of Calgary Press, 2004.

Comfort, Darlene J. *The Abasand Fiasco: The Rise and Fall of a Brave Pioneer Oil Sands Extraction Plant*. Edmonton: Friesen Printers, 1980.

Cross, Philip, and Geoff Bowlby. *The Alberta Economic Juggernaut: The Boom on the Rose*. Canadian Economic Observer, September 2006, Statistics Canada, catalogue number 11-010.

de Mille, George. *Oil in Canada West: The Early Years*. Calgary: Northwest Printing and Lithographing, 1970.

Diehl, Fred M. *A Gentleman from a Fading Age: Eric Lafferty Harvie*. Calgary: Devonian Foundation, 1989.

Ells, S.C. *Recollections of the Development of the Athabasca Oil Sands*. Department of Mines and Technical Surveys, Ottawa, July, 1962.

Evans, Rachel. "Deep, Dark Secrets, Oil Well Spies paid up to $1000 a day to Steal Data." *Edmonton Sun*, September 13, 1998, 14.

Ferguson, Barry Glen. *Athabasca Oil Sands: Northern Resource Exploration 1875–1951*. Alberta Culture/ Canadian Plains Research Centre, 1985.

Finch, David. *Hell's Half Acre: Early Days in the Great Alberta Oil Patch*. Surrey, BC: Heritage House, 2005.

Findlay, Alan. "Emissions on the Rise: Made-in-Canada Solution Needed." *Edmonton Sun*, April 8, 2006, 30.

Foster, Peter. *The Blue-Eyed Sheiks: The Canadian Oil Establishment*. Toronto: Collins, 1979.

Francis, Diane. "Happiness is never giving up control." *National Post*, June 21, 2001.

George, Rick, president and CEO, Suncor. Interview, June 20, 2006.

Gray, Earle. *The Great Canadian Oil Patch: The Petroleum Era from Birth to Peak*. 2nd ed. Edmonton: June Warren Publishing, 2004.

Henton, Darcy. "Boom a Shock!" *Edmonton Sun*, September 1, 2006, 7.

Hoos, Aaron. "History of the Alberta Oil and Gas Industry, Part One: Kootenai Brown." *Alberta Oil, the Magazine*, Fall 2004, 14–15.

Hoos, Aaron. "Peter Pond: The Man who Helped Put Alberta on the Map." *Alberta Oil, the Magazine*, Spring 2006, 102–104.

Huberman, Irwin. *The Place We Call Home: A History of Fort McMurray as its People Remember*. Fort McMurray: Historical Book Society of Fort McMurray, 2001.

Johnston, Bart. "Is Well Blaster an Ex-Pastor?" *Edmonton Sun*, August 26, 1998, 3.

Kerr, Aubrey. *Leduc*. Edmonton: Friesen Printers, 1991.

Kerr, Aubrey. *Redwater*. Calgary: S.A. Kerr, 1994.

Klassen, Henry C. *A Business History of Alberta*. Calgary: University of Calgary Press, 1999.

Koch, George. "Corporate Success, Southern-style." *Alberta Report*, January 9, 1995, 14–17.

Landry, Frank. "Klein Blasts Gore, Premier Defends Alberta's Oilsands Development." *Calgary Sun*, July 5, 2006, 5.

le Riche, Timothy. "Albertans Cashed In." *Edmonton Sun*, March 22, 2006, 56.

le Riche, Timothy. "China Buys into Oilsands." *Edmonton Sun*, June 1, 2005, 44.

le Riche, Timothy. "Fort Mac No Club." *Edmonton Sun*, February 9, 2005, 49.

le Riche, Timothy. "Hydrocarbon Upgrading Task Force." *Alberta Oil, the Magazine*, Volume 1, Issue 3, 2005, 42–43.

le Riche, Timothy. "Oil and Ingenuity." *Edmonton Sun*, December 28, 1999, 64.

le Riche, Timothy. "Paris-based Total SA adds French Flavour to the Alberta Oil Sands." *Alberta Oil, the Magazine*, Volume 2, Issue 1, 2005, 68.

le Riche, Timothy. "Signs of the Times." *Edmonton Sun*, June 3, 2006, 72.

Lorenz, Andrea. "The House that Clay Built." *OilWeek*, November 1, 2004.

Lowey, Mark. "An Interview with Roger Butler." *Alberta Oil, the Magazine*, Volume 2, Issue 2, 2006, 33.

Lyon, Jim. *Dome: The Rise and Fall of the House that Jack Built*. Toronto: Macmillan, 1983.

Macleod, R.C., ed. *William Stewart Herron: Father of the Petroleum Industry in Alberta*. Calgary: Historical Society of Alberta, 1984.

"Man From Medicine Hat, The." *Time*, February 18, 1974.

Martin, Don. *King Ralph: The Political Life and Success of Ralph Klein*. Toronto: Key Porter Books, 2003.

Martin, Sandra. "Bill Hopper, Oilman 1933–2006." *Globe & Mail*, July 8, 2006, S13.

Maudie, Max. "$2 Billion Sought for Explosive Growth." *Edmonton Sun*, September 16, 2006, 8.

National Energy Program, Energy, Mines and Resources Canada, 1980.

Newell, Eric, former Syncrude president. Interview June 1, 2006.

Nikiforuk, Andrew. *Saboteurs: Wiebo Ludwig's War Against Big Oil*. Toronto: Mcfarlane, Walter & Ross, 2001.

Nikiforuk, Andrew. "Saint or Sinner?" *Canadian Business*, May 13, 2002, 54–60.

"Northern Nukes: an Oil Sands Solution?" *Alberta Oil, the Magazine*, Volume 1, Issue 3, 2005, 25–27.

Ogonoski, Paula. "Prince Philip tours the oilsands." *Fort McMurray Today*, May 25, 2005.

"Petro Windfall." *Edmonton Sun*, October 2, 2004, 75.

Phillips, Ed. *Guts & Guile: True Tales from the Back Rooms of the Pipeline Industry*. Vancouver: Douglas & McIntyre, 1990.

Rowat, Miles Ryan. *Boom Times: Canada's Crude Petroleum Industry*. Statistics Canada, September 2006, catalogue number 11-621-MIE2006047.

Remington, Robert. "Released Hostages Tell of Nightmare." *National Post*, December 23, 1999, A9.

Sheppard, Mary Clark. *Oil Sands Scientist: The Letters of Karl. A. Clark*. Edmonton: University of Alberta Press, 1989.

"Sixty Minutes Booster." *Edmonton Sun*, January 24, 2006, 46.

Stinson, Douglas. "It Takes Two Tonnes of Oil Sands." *Alberta Oil, the Magazine*, Volume 1, Issue 4, 2005, 25.

"Texas of the North," *Time*, Sept. 24, 1951.

Wilson, Ian. "Alberta Hit Hard After NEP Introduced." *Edmonton Sun*, October 29, 2005, 79.

Wilson, Ian. "Energy Boss Hints at Revolt," *Edmonton Sun*, November 15, 2006, 82.

Wilson, Ian. "Lougheed Turned Off the Taps." *Edmonton Sun*, October 31, 2005, 47.

Wilson, Ian. "NEP was Avoidable: Lalonde." *Edmonton Sun*, October 28, 2005, 63.

Wilson, Ian. "Piece of the Pie." *Edmonton Sun*, October 29, 2005, 79.

Wilson, Ian. "Shaken Trust," *Edmonton Sun*, November 2, 2006, 8.

Wood, David G. *The Lougheed Legacy*. Toronto: Key Porter Books, 1985.

www.alliance-pipeline.com

www.atco.com

www.canadianbusiness.com

www.cren.ca/content_view2

www.enbridge.com/about/corporateOverview/historical-highlights.php

www.encana.com

www.exploration-processing.com/content_archives/Fall05/06.html

www.fhoa.ca/1920tv.htm

hellshalfacres.com/drupal/node/view/1200

www.imperialoil.ca/Canada-English/ThisIs/Story/TI_S_1880.asp

www.neb-one.gc.ca/EnergyReports/EMAOilSandsSupply-Market2015Canada2000_e.pdf

www.nickles.com/history/

www.oilsandsdiscovery.com/oil_sands_story/pdfs/bitu-mount.pdf

www.petro-canada.ca

www.shell.ca

www.suncor.com

www.syncrude.ca/investors/speeches24.html

www.town.devon.ab.ca/about/history.aspx

www.turnervalley.ca/history.htm

TIMOTHY LE RICHE

After high school, Timothy le Riche spent a year working in the Nisku yard of S&T Drilling, building rigs, stacking pipe and generally getting filthy. Today, as business editor of the *Edmonton Sun*, he often writes about Alberta's energy industry, particularly the oil sands. He has been on staff at the *Sun* for 20 years. This is his second book for Folklore Publishing. Tim also writes for trade magazines. In his spare time, he coaches his sons' basketball teams.